PUNISHMENT AS SOCIETAL-DEFENSE

Studies in Social, Political, and Legal Philosophy
General Editor: James P. Sterba, University of Notre Dame

PUNISHMENT AS SOCIETAL-DEFENSE

Phillip Montague

ROWMAN & LITTLEFIELD PUBLISHERS, INC.

ROWMAN & LITTLEFIELD PUBLISHERS, INC.

Published in the United States of America
by Rowman & Littlefield Publishers, Inc.
4720 Boston Way, Lanham, Maryland 20706

3 Henrietta Street
London WC2E 8LU, England

British Cataloging in Publication Information Available

Library of Congress Cataloging-in-Publication Data
Montague, Phillip
Punishment as societal defense / Phillip Montague.
p.   cm.—(Studies in social, political, and legal
philosophy)
Includes index.
1. Capital punishment—Moral and ethical aspects.   2. Capital
punishment—Government policy.   3. Criminal justice, Administration
of—Moral and ethical aspects.   4. Discrimination in capital
punishment.   I. Title.   II. Series.
HV8693.M66   1995   364.6′01—dc20   95-22351   CIP

ISBN 0–8476–8071–1 (cloth: alk. paper)
ISBN 0–8476–8072–X (pbk.: alk. paper)

Printed in the United States of America

∞ TM   The paper used in this publication meets the minimum requirements of
American National Standard for Information Sciences—Permanence of
Paper for Printed Library Materials, ANSI Z39.48–1984.

for Margo and Nicole

Contents

Author's Note

Part of Chapter Two appeared in a slightly different version in Phillip Montague, "Self-Defense and Choosing Between Lives," *Philosophical Studies*, 40 (1981) (Copyright 1981 by D. Reidel Publishing Co., Dordrecht, Holland, and Boston, U.S.A.). Material reprinted by permission of Kluwer Academic Publishers.

Part of Chapter Three appeared in a slightly different version in Phillip Montague, "Punishment and Societal Defense," *Criminal Justice Ethics* 2 (1983) (Copyright 1983, The Institute for Criminal Justice Ethics). Material reprinted by permission of the Institute for Criminal Justice Ethics.

Introduction

As an understandable response to crime rates that appear to be rising swiftly and inexorably, many people are placing increased emphasis on the punishment of criminal wrongdoers. This increased emphasis on legal punishment has not only revitalized timeworn debates concerning the morality of capital punishment, but it has also stimulated controversies about the morality of legal punishment in general. While many of the issues commonly raised in connection with capital punishment are issues of principle, however, those most frequently raised in relation to legal punishment in general are practical in nature. Thus, people who object to the death penalty typically do so on the principled ground that capital punishment infringes rights everyone has not to be killed, and is therefore simply a form of unjustified homicide, while proponents of the death penalty commonly insist that moral principles require that perpetrators of particularly heinous crimes be executed. In contrast, more general moral concerns about legal punishment tend to presuppose that punishing wrongdoers (in certain ways, at least) is justified in principle, and they focus on questions about crowded prisons, the appropriateness of treating teenage perpetrators of violent crimes as adults, possible racist influences in sentencing, and so on.

There is, of course, a long tradition that recognizes that punishment need not be lethal to generate serious problems of moral principle. A central component of this tradition is the idea that *all* standard forms of legal punishment can reasonably be regarded as harming the persons punished and, perhaps, as infringing certain of their rights, and as therefore at least presumptively objectionable from a moral standpoint. According to this way of thinking, if executing murderers infringes their rights not to be killed, imprisoning thieves, rapists, and muggers infringes their rights not to be involuntarily confined; if the practice of capital punishment generates a justification problem because of its harmful character, then so does the practice of legal punishment in general.

Now, situations certainly do arise in which people are justified in harming others even if harming them appears to infringe their rights. In particular, people can be justified in harming others when doing so is the only way to defend themselves (or other innocent persons) against wrongful aggression. If the contexts in which societies impose punishments are appropriately analogous to those in which individuals perform acts of self-defense, then the considerations that justify harming others in the latter contexts might also justify harming people through punishment.

This line of thinking, while intuitively appealing (and acknowledged as such by a number of writers over the years), is seriously problematic in two respects, however. First of all, even if there is some basis on which to view legal punishment as a vehicle for societal-defense, the analogy between self-defense and societal-defense seems to fail at a crucial point. For whereas in justified acts of self-defense, harming people is the only way in which they can be prevented from harming others, people are punished for harm that they have already inflicted on innocent persons. A second problem associated with attempting to justify punishment on the basis of purported analogies between legal punishment and self defense is that explaining the moral dimensions of self-defense is itself notoriously difficult.

Hence, achieving the goal of this book—which is to provide a societal-defense account of the justifiability of legal punishment—requires that two tasks be accomplished. The first is that of providing a plausible and well-developed theory of individual self-defense, and the second is that of constructing the requisite analogy between self-defense on the one hand, and legal punishment (understood as a mechanism for societal-defense) on the other. After presenting a brief overview of the problem of justifying legal punishment and traditional approaches to solving this problem in chapter one, I undertake the first of these tasks in chapter two, where the morality of individual self-defense is examined and explained. I undertake the second task—that of constructing the analogy between self- and societal-defense—in chapter three. As I noted above, accomplishing this latter task requires (among other things) explaining how there can be such an analogy when it appears that acts of self-defense occur before harm is done to innocent people, while legal punishment is after the fact.

Explaining punishment as societal defense is regarded here as involving not only a presentation of the theory itself, but also an examination of certain alternative approaches to justifying legal punishment. The two alternatives briefly discussed in chapter one—traditional deterrence and retributivist theories—are quite familiar. I examine less familiar variations on deterrence and retributivist themes in chapter four, and consider a very different type of view, centering on the idea of a societal right to punish, in chapter five. A main purpose of these discussions of alternatives to the theory of punishment as societal-defense is to illuminate this latter theory by providing bases for comparison and contrast.

A second purpose of the discussions of alternatives to punishment as societal-defense is to emphasize the importance of finding an appropriate home in moral theory for certain considerations that are relevant to the morality of legal punishment. If an account of the morality of legal punishment is to have any chance at all of being complete and satisfactory, then it must not only identify the moral principles relevant to determining the moral status of legal punishment, but it must also explain how these principles are related to more general moral considerations. Recognition of this need motivates the discussions of justice that take place in chapters two and three, and also for the extended examination of rights that occurs in chapter five. The former discussions center on a certain principle that concerns the just distribution of burdens in contexts that include both self-defense and societal-defense—contexts to which more familiar principles of justice are inapplicable.

As this last remark suggests, here we interpret justifying punishment as a problem of distributive justice. But because the principle of distributive justice that underlies punishment as societal-defense incorporates backward-looking considerations similar to those associated with retributive theories, it erases the sharp line some writers draw between distributive and retributive justice. And by linking the justification problem for punishment in morally significant ways with other—seemingly independent—problems of distributive justice, the theory of punishment as societal-defense acquires theoretical underpinnings of a sort required for any account of the morality of punishment to be acceptable.

The book's final chapter examines the morality of capital punishment. The purpose of this chapter is twofold: to argue on grounds of societal-defense that establishing systems of punishment that contain the death penalty is justifiable in principle; and to consider certain practical difficulties associated with justifying the inclusion of capital punishment in actual systems of punishment. In this latter connection, special attention is devoted to the moral significance of racial influences on sentencing decisions in capital cases. And, in pursuing a resolution of this issue, the discussion centers once more on questions about the nature of justice—questions that are answered in light of an explanation of the relevance of comparative considerations to matters of justice in the distribution of benefits and burdens.

Chapter 1

Background

The Justification Problem

One might suppose that a discussion of the justifiability of punishment should attempt early on to define "punishment" since, one might further suppose, fruitfully examining the morality of punishment is impossible without an understanding of what punishment is. While this latter suggestion is certainly correct, however, it does not support the former. For one does not require a definition of "punishment" in order to recognize clear cases of punishment's being imposed and to distinguish such cases from those in which individuals are treated in ways that, although similar to punishment in certain respects, are nevertheless something else entirely.

For example, imprisonment, quarantine, and civil commitment can all involve involuntary confinement, but only the first is punishment. And while both imprisonment and threats of imprisonment can be coercive, threatening people with punishment is not the same as punishing them. To be sure, not everything that bears the label "punishment" clearly is punishment, and not everything from which the designation "punishment" is commonly withheld clearly falls outside the realm of what punishment actually is. However, our concern here is with *clear* cases, and with the moral issues they generate.

Although these clear cases can be found in a wide variety of contexts, our sole concern here is with the punishments that societies impose on those of their members who engage in certain types of legally prohibited activities or who fail to act in ways required of them by law. Such "legal punishments" occur within (typically complex) institutional frameworks that specify the types of acts counted as offenses and the punishments those acts call for, the procedures by which offenders are to be identified and punished, and so on. As we will see, justifying the

1

existence of such frameworks—with their diverse components—is an important part of justifying (legal) punishment.

The most controversial form of legal punishment is, of course, the death penalty. Opponents of capital punishment commonly argue that, by executing people convicted of certain offenses, societies "lower themselves" to the criminals' level by doing exactly what the latter are being punished for. The "lowering" here is clearly regarded as moral in nature: societies sentence people to death for having acted in seriously immoral ways, for having killed other people in particular, and then societies act in those very same immoral ways when they carry out death sentences. If this line of reasoning works against capital punishment, then we can presumably generalize it so that it applies in a similar way to other forms of punishment. The more general argument goes like this: the acts that are commonly punishable by law are acts that fit under the headings of "serious wrongs" and "infringements of important moral rights"; yet the punishments imposed for the performance of such acts (punishments that involve things such as confining people against their will, and depriving them of property and privacy) are of types that wrong people and infringe their rights in normal circumstances.

That is, the acts *for* which people are punished, and the acts *by* which they are punished—although seeming somehow to differ significantly from each other—are disturbingly similar in morally relevant respects. If we agree, for example, that murderers infringe their victims' rights to life, then are we not compelled to conclude that capitally punishing murderers infringes their rights to life? Similarly, if we say that kidnappers infringe important rights when they forcibly relocate and confine their victims, then are not those very same rights infringed when kidnappers are arrested and imprisoned? In short, how can societies possibly be justified in punishing even those of their members who engage in the most serious of wrongdoings?

To be sure, the philosophical literature of punishment overflows with proposed answers to this last question, and, while these answers reflect widely varying views regarding the justifiability of punishment, they divide into two major groups. In one group are claims to the effect that, perhaps appearances to the contrary notwithstanding, rights are *not* infringed when wrongdoers are punished—call this the "no-infringement view." The other group comprises variations on the theme that, although wrongdoers' rights *are* infringed when they are punished, the infringements are permissible or justified—call this the "permissible-infringement view." I have a good deal to say about these two groups of claims later, but it is useful at this point to look briefly at some of the more prominent members of each group.

The no-infringement view might take the form of maintaining that wrongdoers *forfeit* certain of their rights when they engage in their wrongdoing—something that is commonly said of murderers by proponents of capital punishment. This way of thinking seems to assume that various types of criminal behavior result in the forfeiture of specific rights, and yet there is no obvious way to identify the rights that are purportedly forfeited when particular types of immoral acts are performed. Thus, while it might seem reasonable to say that murderers forfeit their right to life, and that kidnappers forfeit their right to not be confined against their wishes, this neat correspondence is missing in the case of robbers, rapists, and vandals. The difficulty here is plainly reminiscent of the familiar problem faced by anyone who espouses the more general position that punishments should fit crimes in the sense that the former should *match* the latter.

The more basic question that this view invites, however, is whether rights such as the right to life and not to be confined against one's wishes can be forfeited. There is, after all, a long and respectable tradition according to which such rights are inalienable. And, while this tradition might be mistaken, we cannot reasonably dismiss it out of hand. In any case, it is surely incumbent on proponents of the forfeiture view to argue for their position. And, since some accounts of rights (such as the one to be developed in chapter five) do not easily accommodate the idea of forfeiture, those employing this idea must argue in light of a well-developed and plausible theory of rights.

A second form of the no-infringement view centers on the claim that no one possesses, say, rights to life, privacy, and liberty; rather, they possess the right to life only if . . . , the right to privacy only if . . . , and the right to liberty only if. . . . A proponent of this position would presumably claim that people possess a right to life only if (perhaps among other things) they do not murder other people, from which we could not infer that rights to life are infringed when murderers are executed.

The difficulties associated with this way of thinking about rights parallel in certain respects those surrounding the forfeiture view just discussed. Thus, while it might seem reasonable to say that people have a right to life only if they have not committed murder, not only is it very unclear whether any additional qualifications are associated with the right to life, but it is also difficult to identify the qualifications that should be thought of as applicable to other rights. How, for example, should we fill the blanks in ''People have a right to not be forcibly confined only if . . .'' and ''People have a right to privacy only if. . . .''[1]

Faced with the serious difficulties that surround these versions of the no-infringement view (and in the absence of plausible alternative versions), we might be attracted to some form of the permissible-infringement view. That is, we might find attractive the idea that, while wrongdoers' rights are indeed infringed when they are punished, these infringements are permissible. But this sort of view has problems of its own.

These problems arise from certain reasonable claims regarding the interrelations among rights, obligations, and permissions. The relevant claims are these: (1) if people have a right not to be treated in a certain sort of way, then others are obligated not to treat them in that sort of way;[2] and (2) if people are permitted to perform actions of a certain type, then they are not obligated to refrain from performing actions of that type. Assume now that people have a right not to be forcibly confined—from which it follows that, given (1), others are obligated not to confine them. Assume too that forcibly confining wrongdoers by imprisoning them is morally permissible, so that, given (2), refraining from imprisoning them is not obligatory. We can then conclude that refraining from imprisoning people is obligatory, and also that refraining from imprisoning them is not obligatory, and this result certainly seems to be contradictory.

One approach to avoiding this problem with the permissible-infringement view relies on the distinction between presumptive (defeasible, prima facie) rights on the one hand, and strict (indefeasible, actual) rights on the other; and on the parallel distinctions between presumptive and strict obligations, and presumptive and strict permissions. The idea is that, by drawing such a distinction within the area of rights, the permissible-infringement view does not generate contradictions. And, with the problem of contradictions eliminated, the permissible-infringement view warrants serious consideration. This way of thinking about rights is presupposed in discussions of versions of the permissible-infringement view—which versions include the societal-defense account of punishment to be developed and defended in this book.[3]

Justifying punishment by way of the permissible-infringement view would require identifying considerations in virtue of which the (presumptive) rights of wrongdoers can be permissibly infringed; and versions of the permissible-infringement view differ from each other according to how they characterize these considerations. However, underlying all forms of the permissible-infringement view is the idea that, because punishing people infringes their rights, there are good moral reasons against punishment; and punishing offenders is justified only if there are countervailing better reasons in favor of doing so. Traditionally, two views regarding the nature of these countervailing reasons have occupied center stage. On the one hand, we have retributivism in its various forms, according to which the justifiability of punishment is determined (in the final analysis) by certain "backward-looking" considerations—by considerations of moral desert in particular. And, on the other hand, we have deterrence theories, according to which the justifiability of punishment is a "forward-looking" matter, and is determined (in the final analysis) by the deterrent value of punishing people.

Although retributivist and deterrence theories are the most familiar accounts of the justification of punishment, interestingly different rival positions have competed for attention in recent years. One of the more appealing of these centers on the idea that societies (governments, the authorities, etc.) have a right to punish offenders. In this view, when societies infringe rights through punishment, they are themselves *exercising* a certain right. Hence, such situations involve conflicts between society's right to punish and the right of wrongdoers not to be killed, involuntarily confined, and so on; and it must be possible for these conflicts to resolve themselves sometimes in society's favor if the idea of a societal right to punish is to be taken seriously. I examine a particular right-to-punish theory in chapter five.[4]

Punishment as societal-defense—which relies on certain analogies drawn between individual self-defense on the one hand and punishment on the other—is neither a deterrence nor a retributivist theory, nor does it imply the existence of a societal right to punish wrongdoers. Roughly, the idea is that punishment is justified to the extent that it serves appropriately as an instrument of societal-defense—where the moral dimensions of societal-defense are explained as analogous to those of individual self-defense.

We have referred to various philosophical approaches to the problem of justifying legal punishment—and, indeed, various ways in which this problem can be understood. Interpreted most simply, the justification problem is that of explaining how imprisoning people, capitally punishing them, and so on, can be morally permissible. And this is the interpretation under which the justification problem is addressed by certain versions of the no-infringement view—for example, those that amount to little more than the claim that people forfeit certain of their rights by engaging in criminal activity. We noted that these views are seriously problematic, and we will see in chapter five that these problems are inherited by more complex versions of the no-infringement view, which aim at doing more than merely showing that punishment is permissible. Most of our attention, however, will be devoted to examining forms of the permissible-infringement view, all of which will be interpreted as proposing defeasibility conditions for the moral presumption against standard forms of punishment.

The remainder of this chapter is devoted to two forms of the permissible-infringement view referred to above—deterrence theories and retributivism—or, rather, to the most familiar and straightforward versions of these positions. Supporters and critics alike have discussed both of these versions of deterrence and retributivist theories at great length, and the arguments for and against them need not be considered at any length here. These two types of deterrence and retributivist theories do, however, require at least brief consideration before proceeding—and this for two reasons: doing so will provide a framework within which to locate the theory of punishment as societal-defense relative to other theories; and it will assist us in our later examination of less familiar and more sophisticated types of deterrence and retributivist theories.

Utilitarian-based Deterrence Theories

According to deterrence theories, facts about punishment's effectiveness in deterring would-be wrongdoers are—in and of themselves—necessarily relevant to whether punishment is justified.[5] Such theories therefore have two important implications. The first is that, if a punishment is effective in deterring wrongdoing, then its being so is a reason (although perhaps not a conclusive one) for imposing the punishment irrespective of the punishment's other features—irrespective, for example, of whether the punishment is imposed on people guilty of serious wrongdoing. The second noteworthy implication of deterrence theories is that situations cannot possibly arise in which a punishment's deterrent effectiveness is entirely irrelevant to whether the punishment is justified.

As their name implies, utilitarian-based deterrence theories are derived from utilitarian accounts of the nature of morality; and these deterrence theories can therefore be thought of as arising from four enormously plausible—and apparently simple—ideas: that promoting the general welfare is morality's fundamental requirement; that reducing crime promotes the general welfare; that crime can be reduced by credibly threatening potential wrongdoers with punishment, thereby deterring them from engaging in wrongdoing; and that the credibility of such threats is typically established by actually punishing those who ignore them.[6]

As proposals for solving the justification problem for punishment, then, utilitarian-based deterrence theories can be understood as centering on the idea that facts about the deterrent effects of punishing people can defeat moral presumptions against punishing them. The most familiar form of utilitarianism is act utilitarianism, according to which a particular action is right (obligatory, required, and so on) just in case the aggregate value of its consequences is greater than that of the consequences of any alternative action.[7] If we apply this theory to an act of punishing some person, the result is that punishing the person is right just in case the aggregate value of the consequences of punishing her— including the deterrent effectiveness of doing so—is greater than that of the consequences of any alternative action. Let us refer to the deterrence theory that arises from act utilitarianism as "act utilitarianism for punishment."

Although act utilitarianism provides a natural theoretical home for deterrence theories, act utilitarians do not own the concept of deterrence. Proposals for justifying punishment can treat punishment's deterrent effectiveness and other consequences as morally significant without implying that they are its only morally significant features. Such proposals acknowledge that considerations of deterrence are capable of defeating the moral presumption against punishment while regarding other sorts of considerations—even backward-looking ones—as able to fill this role.

Consider first of all rule utilitarianism, according to which an action is right (obligatory, required, and so on) just in case it is prescribed by acceptable moral rules, and moral rules are acceptable just in case they are components of systems, practices, or institutions the establishment and implementation of which yields greater aggregate value than do alternative systems, practices, and institutions. Rule utilitarianism implies that particular acts of punishment are right just in case their rightness follows from the rules of a system of punishment that is justified on utilitarian grounds. Assuming that implementing a system of punishment can have deterrent effects and assuming that the deterrent effects of a system of punishment are necessarily among its desirable consequences, then rule utilitarianism generates a deterrence theory of punishment—a theory that we will refer to as "rule utilitarianism for punishment."

Many punishment theorists have found rule utilitarianism for punish-

ment attractive for at least three reasons. The first is that—in contrast
to act utilitarianism for punishment—the former's double-level justification structure separates two questions regarding the justification of
punishment that are importantly different from each other: one question
concerns the justification of individual punishments, and the other is
about the justifiability of the systems of punishment within which individuals are punished.

A second reason for the appeal of rule utilitarianism for punishment
is that, by not allowing forward-looking considerations—including deterrent value—to be relevant at the level of individual punishment, rule
utilitarianism for punishment reflects the workings of actual systems of
punishment that seem prima facie to be fair. Thus, suppose that a person
is found guilty of murder through the procedures prescribed by a morally acceptable system of punishment, and that the rules of the system
prescribe life imprisonment for murderers. Then the question of
whether the person should be imprisoned for life clearly seems to call
for a "yes" answer—and this without regard for the deterrent effects
of that particular act of punishment.

Third, advocates of rule utilitarianism for punishment see it as capable of avoiding an especially serious difficulty associated with act utilitarianism for punishment by allowing certain backward-looking considerations to be relevant to whether punishment is justified. The following
argument gives some indication of the nature and seriousness of this
difficulty: since act utilitarianism for punishment is entirely forward
looking, it implies that a person's guilt or innocence is at most contingently relevant to whether punishing her is justified; hence, punishing
an innocent person could be morally justified solely by virtue of the
deterrent value of doing so, and without any regard at all for the person's innocence; but considerations of guilt and innocence are necessarily relevant to the justifiability of punishing people, and act utilitarianism for punishment must therefore be rejected.

Although writers on deterrence theories have offered various replies
to this argument—or, rather, to arguments that it superficially resembles—none has been very successful; and, as a result, many of those
sympathetic to deterrence theories have been led to abandon act utilitarianism for punishment in favor of either rule utilitarianism for punishment or some nonutilitarian theory. While we need not spend much
time here examining ways in which proponents of act utilitarianism for
punishment might attempt to counter the argument of the preceding
paragraph, one type of attempt is worth a brief look.[8] This is because
the argument in question needs to be distinguished from a more familiar

and similar-sounding argument; and because both rule utilitarianism for punishment and certain *non*-utilitarian theories are vulnerable to a parallel argument, and advocates of such theories try to avoid its unacceptable implications by means of claims that closely parallel that employed by many who defend act utilitarian justifications of punishment. The pertinent act utilitarian claim is that, fanciful suppositions by philosophers aside, punishing innocent people in the real world does not have better overall consequences than does punishing guilty people, and, hence, act utilitarianism for punishment does not imply that punishing innocent people is justified.

This reply misses its mark, however, since it actually pertains to an argument that differs from its intended target in two respects.

First of all, the argument presented here is not the familiar one that situations can certainly arise in which punishing innocent people has better consequences than alternative actions, and is therefore justifiable on act utilitarian grounds. Rather, it is concerned with the ability of act utilitarianism for punishment even to attribute moral significance—necessary moral significance, that is—to considerations of guilt and innocence.

Second, the antiutilitarian argument advanced above says nothing about the implications of applying act utilitarianism for punishment in the real world. Rather, it focuses on a *theoretical* feature of act utilitarianism for punishment. It states that considerations of guilt and innocence are necessarily relevant to whether punishing people is justified, and that the necessary relevance of these considerations cannot be accounted for by act utilitarianism for punishment. If these claims are true (as they seem clearly to be), then the fact—if it is a fact—that act utilitarianism for punishment does not actually justify punishing innocent people is beside the point. Indeed, a critic of act utilitarianism for punishment might grant that punishing innocent people can be justified in special circumstances, while continuing to maintain that even in these circumstances the innocence of those who are punished creates a moral presumption against punishing them—a presumption that act utilitarianism for punishment cannot accommodate.

The point here is that claims about the actual deterrent value of punishment are irrelevant to the acceptability of act utilitarianism for punishment. As is the case with other deterrence theories—and, indeed, with theories of punishment in general—act utilitarianism for punishment is being construed here as necessarily true if true at all, and as therefore implying nothing about the actual world without the aid of premises that are contingently true if true at all.

Let us now turn our attention to rule utilitarianism for punishment.

Rule utilitarianism for punishment treats forward-looking considerations such as deterrent effectiveness as the only ones relevant to whether systems of punishment (and their varied components) are justified, while attributing moral significance to backward-looking considerations at the level of individual punishment. We noted earlier that rule utilitarianism for punishment is regarded by its proponents as invulnerable to the objections to which act utilitarianism for punishment is open. The idea is that backward-looking considerations (and considerations of guilt and innocence in particular) can be built into systems of punishment, and, in this way, they can become relevant to whether individual punishments are justified. In fact, however, rule utilitarianism for punishment is open to objections that exactly parallel the most serious of those to which act utilitarianism for punishment is vulnerable.

In explaining how this is so, we will find it useful first of all to note a certain difference between the way rule utilitarianism for punishment has been stated here, and the way it is sometimes formulated elsewhere. In discussing the theory, some writers distinguish questions about the justification of individual punishments on the one hand, from questions about "the general justifying aim of the practice of punishment" on the other.[9] These latter questions, while they might well be important, do not arise (at least not directly) from our formulation of rule utilitarianism for punishment. As we have stated the theory, it furnishes a criterion for selecting among possible systems of punishment; and it does so without presupposing that there is any such thing as *the* practice of punishment.

To be sure, one might discuss the general justifying aim of punishment without any mention of "the practice of punishment." Indeed, the theory of punishment developed in chapter three reflects the idea that punishment's general justifying aim is societal-defense. However, the point of proposing a justifying aim for punishment is presumably to use it as a criterion for selecting among systems of punishment—a point that is likely to be obscured by references to *the* practice of punishment. Such systems do, after all, come in various shapes and sizes, and the various components of a system of punishment must presumably be chosen in light of punishment's general justifying aim.

For example, rule utilitarianism for punishment evidently dictates that forward-looking considerations are the only ones necessarily relevant to whether systems of punishment should provide trial by jury; whether they should incorporate a presumption of innocence for people accused of crimes; whether they should contain the death penalty;

whether they should correlate the most severe punishments with the most serious offenses and the least severe punishments with the least serious offenses; and so on. And, according to rule utilitarianism for punishment, forward-looking considerations alone determine whether and, if so, how guilt and innocence should be taken into account—whether, for example, rules allowing the families of offenders to be punished are morally acceptable if their implementation would have great deterrent value.

In other words, according to rule utilitarianism for punishment—as is the case with act utilitarianism for punishment—considerations of guilt and innocence are at most contingently relevant to whether punishment is justified. Given that such considerations are necessarily relevant to how systems of punishment should be constructed, rule utilitarianism for punishment is open to an objection analogous to that which creates the most serious difficulty for act utilitarianism for punishment. The underlying point here is that the moral acceptability of neither individual punishments nor systems of punishment is determined by forward-looking considerations alone.

Before leaving our discussion of utilitarian-based deterrence theories of punishment, some brief remarks about nonutilitarian deterrence theories will provide a useful contrast.

There are, first of all, theories that resemble act utilitarianism for punishment in being single level—in being concerned only with justifying particular acts of punishment—but that treat forward-looking considerations as merely *among* those necessarily relevant to the justifiability of individual acts of punishment. Such a theory might, for example, prohibit punishing innocent people no matter how effectively such punishment would deter wrongdoing. There can also be double-level theories that, because they exhibit a similar eclecticism with respect to the sorts of considerations that are relevant to whether systems of punishment are justified, do not arise from rule utilitarianism. For example, a system of punishment might contain a rule that requires that punishments fit crimes, which rule is justified by appealing to considerations of justice having no necessary confection with the consequences of the rule's being established and implemented. We will have more to say about these nonutilitarian single- and double-level deterrence theories in chapter four.

Desert-based Retributivism

In the preceding section we considered utilitarian versions of deterrence theories, according to which only certain sorts of forward-looking considerations are necessarily relevant to whether acts or systems of punishment are justified. In this section we turn our attention to proposals for justifying punishment on the basis of backward-looking considerations.

Theories of punishment in which backward-looking considerations are necessarily relevant to whether punishment is justified are typically classified as forms of retributivism. However, the precise nature of these backward-looking considerations, as well as their relation to retributivism, are matters of some controversy among philosophers. Thus, some writers focus exclusively on desert, and insist that the essence of retributivism is the link that it forges between a punishment's being justified and its being deserved. Other writers have a very different view of retributivism, however—even some who appear to emphasize desert in their explanations and defenses of retributivism.

According to Jeffrie Murphy, for example, a central component of retributivism is the idea that, "Punishment is justified primarily by backward-looking considerations—i.e., the criminal, having engaged in wrongful conduct in the past, deserves his punishment."[10] Elsewhere, however, Murphy characterizes retributivism in a way that loosens its special ties to desert. In his words,

> The retributive theory of punishment, speaking *very* generally, is a theory that seeks to justify punishment, not in terms of social utility, but in terms of *this* cluster of moral concepts: rights, desert, merit, moral responsibility, justice, and respect for moral autonomy.[11]

Needless to say, the moral concepts to which Murphy refers in these latter remarks comprise an interestingly mixed bag, and theories of punishment based on them will have nothing in common, save for not being derivable from utilitarianism.

Martin Golding distinguishes two types of retributivism—"maximal" and "minimal"—according to whether considerations of desert are treated as sufficient to justify punishment, or as only necessary. That is, whereas minimal retributivists maintain that "one should be punished only if he deserves it,"[12] maximal retributivists hold "not merely that only the guilty should be punished, but also that there is a *duty* to punish someone who is guilty and culpable. . . . Such a person is *deserving* of punishment."[13]

J. L. Mackie also distinguishes two forms of retributivism—"positive" and "negative"—which correspond respectively to Golding's distinction between conditions sufficient and conditions necessary for punishment to be justified; but Mackie explains retributivism without explicit references to desert. He also suggests that retributivism has a "permissive" variety, according to which "one who is guilty may be punished."[14]

Like Mackie, H. L. A. Hart gives no indication that desert is the central concept of retributivism. Hart claims that a retributivist theory

> will assert three things: first, that a person may be punished if, and only if, he has voluntarily done something morally wrong; secondly, that his punishment must in some way match, or be the equivalent of, the wickedness of his offense; and thirdly, that the justification for punishing men under such conditions is that the return of suffering for moral evil voluntarily done, is itself just or morally good.[15]

References to desert are also absent from Hugo Adam Bedau's characterization of retributivism, according to which

> . . . central to the doctrine of . . . retribution in punishment . . . is simply the belief that *justice in punishment requires the features of a punishment to be shaped by reference to features of the offense for which it is meted out.*[16]

Bedau not only explains retributivism without reference to desert, but he also criticizes attempts to characterize retributivism in terms of claims about desert. In his words,

> Probably the most widely held assumption about retribution in punishment is the idea that it makes desert the central feature of just punishment. On this view, a retributivist holds that a punishment is just if and only if the offender deserves it. It seems not to be noticed how essentially trivial this doctrine is; it cannot be central or unique to the theory of retributive punishment. Any theory of the distribution of benefits and burdens, rewards and punishments, can incorporate a notion of desert if it wants to; whatever is said to be properly allocated to (or withheld from) a person under the theory can be said to be deserved (or not deserved) by that person.[17]

We see in these characterizations of retributivism not only different views of how—or even whether—the theory is related to desert, but also different interpretations of the *sort* of account retributivism is. Golding's maximal and minimal retributivisms are, of course, very different sorts of theories; or, rather, maximal retributivism is a candidate for a theory, while minimal retributivism could not count as a theory by itself. The same is true, of course, of Mackie's positive and negative retributivisms. Neither could retributivism be a theory of justification for punishment if interpreted as Bedau suggests it should be; for under Bedau's interpretation, retributivism is at least roughly equivalent to the view that punishments must fit crimes, and it provides nothing in the way of a criterion for determining whether punishment is justified.

In addition, whereas Golding's maximal retributivism (and, arguably, Mackie's positive retributivism) imply that punishment is required under certain conditions, neither Hart's nor Murphy's explanation of retributivism makes any explicit reference to requirements. To be sure, Murphy's characterization of retributivism refers to punishment's being justified, and Hart's refers to its being just. But as we have seen there are proposals for justifying punishment which are concerned only with the *permissibility* of punishment, and Hart's references to the conditions under which a person "may be punished" and to punishment's being "morally good" certainly raise questions about whether he intends his explanation of retributivism to imply anything about a requirement to punish.

These discussions suggest that retributivism is a collection of importantly different views rather than a single, well-defined position. The view of interest to us in this section implies that punishment is morally required under certain conditions, and that the basis of this requirement consists in the fact that wrongdoers deserve punishment. As we will see in chapter four, a retributivist theory might contain desert as an essential component without treating it as *basic*. Thus, some retributivists equate justified punishments with fair punishments; and they regard such appeals to fairness as basic and as furnishing grounds for claims about desert. For example, after explaining retributivism in terms of desert in the remarks quoted above, Murphy defends retributivism by appealing to the "basic principle . . . that no person should profit from his own wrongdoing,"[18] together with the claim that "retribution keeps this from happening."[19] He goes on to say, "If a person does profit from his own wrongdoing . . . this is *unfair* or *unjust*";[20] and it is unjust not only to victims of the wrongdoing, but also to all law-abiding citizens. George Sher defends a version of retributivism based on fairness (a view not unlike Murphy's) in his thoughtful book on the topic of desert.[21] As will become clear later, however, Murphy's and Sher's explanations and defenses of retributivism in terms of fairness are essentially independent of the concept of desert, and one must therefore wonder why their theories should be regarded as genuinely retributivist in nature.

Our concern in this section is with retributivist theories that attempt to justify punishment on the *basis* of claims about desert. As we will be interpreting these desert-based accounts, they regard justified punishments as required rather than merely permitted; and they are maximal or positive rather than minimal or negative. We will ignore the latter forms of retributivism because their implication that punishing innocent people is never justified clearly seems to be too strong. It is surely possible for circumstances to arise in which punishing innocent people is justified, even if such circumstances rarely, if ever, arise in the actual world. If minimal retributivism's requirement that innocent people not be punished were weakened—say, by interpreting it as presumptive—then the resulting theory would be similar in all morally relevant respects to the sort of maximal retributivism that we will be examining.

More precisely, we will understand desert-based retributivism as centering on the following proposition:

(R) Justice requires that people who deliberately engage in certain sorts of wrongdoing be punished, and this based on the fact that such people deserve to be punished. Moreover, given the nature of deserts, the types of punishments imposed on wrongdoers must correspond appropriately to the character of their wrongdoings.

We will interpret the requirements in R as presumptive: R implies that considerations of desert provide presumptive reasons for suitably punishing wrongdoers and that, as such, they can defeat moral presumptions against standard forms of punishment. Moreover, although principles like R are sometimes claimed by their advocates to be so intuitively obvious as to need no justification, we do not take this position here. Accordingly, let us now consider how R might be supported. Doing so clearly will require an examination of the nature of desert.

If people could deserve treatments only within institutional frameworks—if there were no such thing as extrainstitutional *moral* desert—then there would be no chance of producing a basic justification for legal punishment by appealing to desert. In the absence of any very good arguments against the existence of moral deserts, however, we will assume that there are such things; and the task before us is that of determining whether moral desert can provide a basis for retributivism understood according to R. Given how we are interpreting R, we must determine whether considerations of desert can appropriately defeat moral presumptions against punishment—and whether they can do so in a manner that produces an appropriate fit between punishments and wrongdoings.

Before proceeding further, we must acknowledge a distinction that has been ignored to this point. The distinction—which will be explained in greater detail in chapter five—is between two ways in which presumptive obligations can be defeated by conflicting considerations—between "prescriptive" and "permissive" defeaters. If, say, you are presumptively obligated to refrain from performing some action, and if this obligation is defeated by a conflicting presumptive *obligation*, then, other things being equal, you are strictly obligated to act. But if your presumptive obligation to refrain is defeated by one of your presumptive *rights*, then, other things being equal, you are strictly permitted but not obligated to act. In the former circumstance, your presumptive obligation is *prescriptively* defeated, while in the latter it is *permissibly* defeated.

Note now that, while deserts might imply prescriptive or permissive defeaters, they cannot *be* defeaters—at least not in the way that, say, rights and obligations can be. To see this, consider a situation in which you are presumptively obligated to refrain from according someone a certain treatment T. The moral presumption against your according the person T might be defeated either prescriptively or permissibly by a conflicting moral presumption. If the moral presumption against your acting is defeated by a presumptive obligation on your part, then, in the absence of other morally relevant considerations, you are strictly obligated to accord the person T. If, on the other hand, the presumption against your acting is defeated by a right of yours to accord the person T, then, other things being equal, you are strictly permitted to act.

But these intrapersonal conflicts between moral presumptions—between two of your presumptive obligations, or between a presumptive obligation and a presumptive right of yours—stand in sharp contrast to any interpersonal conflict that might exist between *your* presumptive obligation to refrain from according the person treatment T and *that person's* deserving to be accorded T. Moreover, it appears that, if there is indeed an interpersonal conflict between moral presumptions in the latter circumstance, it is parasitic on a more basic intrapersonal conflict. There would be such an intrapersonal conflict between moral presumptions if, say, the other person's deserving the treatment implied that you are presumptively obligated or otherwise required to accord her the treatment.

We might consider, then, whether one person's deserts imply presumptive obligations in others. If deserts do indeed imply such obligations, then a person's deserving punishment would presumably imply that there is an obligation to punish the person. This sort of result would

move us some distance toward justifying R—and hence retributivism—in terms of claims about the nature of desert.

Sher's position on desert comes close to the one we are presently
exploring, although he stops short of claiming that deserts imply obligations. According to Sher, deserts (or "desert-claims") have "normative
force," which includes

> any significant implication that something ought, or ought not to be the
> case. Given this stipulation, a desert-claim will . . . have normative force
> if a specific person (or arm of society) is obligated to provide the deserving
> party with what he deserves. But a claim will also have normative force if
> the deserving party's having what he deserves would, for reasons con-
> nected with the basis of the desert, be an especially good thing.[22]

Hence, for Sher's idea of the normative force of desert to be useful in
establishing R, both the following propositions would have to be true:
that desert claims do indeed have normative force, and that some desert
claims—including claims about deserved punishments—have the sort
of normative force that is associated with moral *requirements* and *prescriptive* defeaters. We will accept the first of these propositions as true
without argument, and focus our attention on the second. Hence—given
how broadly Sher interprets normative force—we will be neither en-
dorsing nor disputing the idea that considerations of desert can function
as *permissive* defeaters. We will not do so because (except for Mackie's
passing reference to permissive retributivism) this idea has played no
explicit role in discussions of retributivism. We will, however, raise
a number of questions about the possibility of interpreting deserts as
prescriptive defeaters. The expression "strictly normative deserts" will
be adopted as a label for any deserts that are capable of functioning as
prescriptive defeaters.

Note first of all that certain deserts are definitely not strictly normative. For example, a person might deserve credit for having lived an
exemplary life without anyone's being required—even presumptively
so—to act in a way that counts as giving the person credit for the life
he has led. People can deserve criticism, praise, or blame for their actions even though no one is required to criticize, praise, or blame them
for what they have done.

Yet, one might insist, it seems completely obvious that some deserts
are strictly normative, and one who subscribes to this position might
attempt to support it with the following line of reasoning.

Suppose that you offer a ten-dollar reward for the return of your lost cat and that some person finds the cat and returns it to you. If the person deserves the offered reward, then you are surely required (presumptively, that is) to pay it to him. Similarly, if an employee of yours satisfies the criteria governing advancement that you have stipulated, then if she deserves to be promoted, you are obligated to promote her. Since you are obligated to treat people according to their deserts, some deserts are strictly normative.

One who believes in strictly normative deserts might go on to suggest that a plausible criterion for distinguishing deserts that are strictly normative from those that are not is easy to produce. We might be urged to note that, in some cases, people simply deserve certain treatments, and in these cases the deserts are not strictly normative, while in other cases they deserve treatments *from others*, and in these cases the deserts are strictly normative. For example (this line of thinking continues), the person imagined as deserving credit for leading a particularly good life does not deserve credit *from* anyone; and the same is generally true for people who deserve criticism, praise, or blame for what they do. In contrast, the person who deserves a ten-dollar reward for returning your lost cat deserves it *from you*—as does your employee who deserves a promotion.

To be sure, as our imaginary proponent of strictly normative deserts might concede, this criterion for distinguishing strictly normative deserts from other deserts is of little or no explanatory value, and it cannot be used to settle problem cases such as that of punishment. That is, since the concern here is with extrainstitutional moral deserts, the question of whether deserved punishments are necessarily deserved from someone or something has no obvious answer. For the proposed criterion to be useful in determining whether particular sorts of deserved treatments are strictly normative, it would have to be supplemented by an explanation of why some treatments are deserved from someone or something, while others are not. Nevertheless, the proposal continues, what has been said so far provides the makings of a plausible account of strictly normative deserts.

Despite its apparent plausibility, however, this account of strictly normative deserts is fundamentally mistaken. Indeed, there is no such thing as a strictly normative desert. The error in thinking that deserts can be strictly normative is best revealed by considering a class of cases to which Sher devotes considerable attention and that seem to exemplify strictly normative deserts. These are cases in which people owe compensation to those whom they have wrongfully caused to suffer losses—as vandals owe compensation to the people whose property they have damaged. Since providing compensation in these cases is obligatory, if the compensation is deserved—as Sher claims it is—then there is reason to regard the desert as strictly normative.

To see what is wrong with this line of thinking, we need first of all to highlight a feature of desert whose existence is almost universally acknowledged in discussions of this topic. Sher alludes to this feature when he says that all desert-claims "have a common structure, in that they all assert that some person or thing deserves some occurrence or mode of treatment in virtue of some fact about him or it. Schematically, they all display the form 'M deserves X for A.' "[23] Sher goes on to say that the values taken by A in "M deserves X for A" are references to past acts or omissions or character traits of M, or something that "falls somewhere in between."[24] Borrowing terminology from Joel Feinberg, he refers to these values of A as "desert-bases."

Although Sher does not make the point, it seems reasonable to regard desert bases as related to normative force in this way: if M deserves X for A, then M ought to be provided with X (or it would be good to provide M with X, and so on) at least in part because of A. If, for example, the person who returns your lost cat deserves the offered reward, then he deserves it for having gone out of his way to return the animal, and you ought to reward him at least partly in virtue of his having gone out of his way to return the cat.

Now consider a situation in which one person (Ann) wrongfully damages the property of another (Bill). Ann is clearly obligated to compensate Bill for the losses she inflicts on him; but for Bill to deserve the compensation, an appropriate desert basis must be present. There must be something about Bill's past acts or about his character in virtue of which he deserves compensation—something that also helps explain why the compensation is owed. But there are no facts about Bill that satisfy these conditions. The only facts about him that have any bearing at all on whether Ann owes him compensation are facts about Bill's *rights*. Hence, the only way to make sense of the idea that Bill deserves compensation from Ann is by regarding Bill's rights as constituting the desert basis in this case. In other words, it would have to be true that Bill deserves compensation from Ann by virtue of Bill's having certain rights, by virtue of those rights having been infringed, etc.

Not only would this interpretation of the desert basis in our example run counter to the plausible and widely accepted idea—one that, as we have noted, is endorsed by Sher—that desert bases are at least related to past acts or character traits of deserving parties, but appeals to Bill's rights render claims about his deserts entirely superfluous. That is, the moral dimensions of the case can be explained as follows: in damaging Bill's property, Ann infringes Bill's property rights, and she thereby incurs an obligation to Bill to compensate him for his losses; and Ann's obligation to compensate Bill corresponds to a right on Bill's part that Ann compensate him.

This explanation locates Ann's obligation to compensate Bill and Bill's right to be compensated within the categories of special obligations and special rights, respectively. People incur special obligations when they voluntarily act in certain ways—when they make promises or borrow money, for example. When people do incur special obligations, they confer special rights on others—rights to have promises kept, to be repaid and so on.[25] The moral dimensions of the case under consideration can be accounted for by invoking these two notions without any references whatever to deserts on Bill's part. Compensation is deserved only in very special circumstances—only if those who have rights to compensation possess features that correspond to the desert bases in more common desert contexts.[26]

Now let us return to our earlier examples which seemed at the time to be cases of strictly normative deserts.

If the person who returns your cat deserves the ten-dollar reward, then this is by virtue of his having returned the cat, and, arguably, of his having gone out of his way to do so, and, again arguably, of his having acted with altruistic motives. But you are presumptively obligated to pay him the ten dollars by virtue of your having offered the reward, thereby conferring a right to be paid ten dollars on anyone who returns the cat. Your obligation is unrelated to the other person's deserts—as is revealed by the fact that the origin of your obligation is explained by appealing to your offering the reward and the fact that you are obligated to pay the person ten dollars even if he doesn't deserve a reward.[27]

Similar remarks apply to the employee whom you are obligated to promote. In establishing promotion criteria, you commit yourself to promoting those of your employees who meet them, and those who do satisfy the criteria have rights against you to be promoted. All this is true regardless of whether the employee deserves to be promoted by virtue of facts about her that might have nothing to do with the promotion criteria. Most of us are, after all, familiar with cases in which people have rights to benefits such as promotions but don't deserve them.[28]

The following summarizes what we have concluded so far about strictly normative deserts: Cases in which people owe others compensation for wrongfully causing them to suffer losses and that Sher claimed to involve deserved compensation, typically have noting whatever to do with deserts. The morally significant features normally possessed by these cases are special obligations of compensation arising from the infringement of certain rights, property rights in particular, and special rights to compensation that correspond to those special obligations. In other cases people do deserve treatments that others are obligated to accord them, but the obligations are unrelated to the deserts and arise from the voluntary performance of certain sorts of acts. In these cases the treatments that people deserve are also treatments to which they have rights, and the deserts and rights are independent of each other.

The question that now confronts us is whether there are *clear* cases that satisfy the following conditions: people are obligated to accord others treatments that the latter deserve, and the deserts or their bases must be appealed to in explaining the existence of the obligations. If there are such cases, then there is reason to believe in strictly normative deserts, and the idea that deserved punishments are strictly normative can be pursued. If there are no such cases, however, then no further attention should be devoted to the issue of whether deserved punishments are strictly normative. If there are no strictly normative deserts, then R—and, with it, desert-based retributivism—should be rejected.

If we eliminate cases in which people obligate themselves to provide deserved treatments, thereby conferring rights to those treatments on the deserving parties, then we might be tempted to look for strictly normative deserts in contexts where deserved treatments are called for by the rules of various types of institutions. If, for example, some person deserves the Nobel Prize in medicine, then she ought presumably to receive the prize, and particular individuals are probably obligated to award the prize to whoever deserves it. There is reason to doubt, however, that the deserts in these contexts are indeed strictly normative, since obligations to provide deserved treatments in institutional contexts clearly seem to arise not from the deserts themselves, but from the rules of the institutions. That is, if someone deserves the Nobel Prize in medicine, then this is by virtue of facts about her and her past actions, but if there are persons who are obligated to award the prize to deserving persons, then they are so obligated by virtue of their institutional roles.

Having concluded that strictly normative deserts are unlikely to be found in contexts involving either special or institutional obligations, where else might we look for them?

Some indication of the paucity of our options in this regard is given by the following list, offered by Joel Feinberg, of major types of deserved treatments,

1. Awards of prizes
2. Assignments of grades
3. Rewards and punishments
4. Praise, blame, and other informal responses
5. Reparation, liability, and other modes of compensation[29]

As Feinberg himself acknowledges, this list might well be incomplete. If it is, however, its omissions are by no means obvious and examining it is instructive. We have seen that the deserts in category 5 are not strictly normative. If there are obligations to award prizes or assign grades, then they are institutional or quasi-institutional in character and are independent of whether the prizes or grades are deserved—a result that casts considerable doubt on the idea that the deserts in categories 1 and 2 are strictly normative. The punishments to which category 3 refers obviously cannot be assumed to be strictly normative on pain of begging the question. We are, therefore, left with rewards and with praise, blame, and "other informal responses."

In fact, only some rewards are viable candidates for the strictly normative deserts we are seeking. Rewards in cases such as that of your lost cat have already been eliminated from consideration, as have rewards that are tied to the workplace or to certain sorts of institutions. Are there deserved rewards that are of neither of these types? Feinberg refers to the reward deserved by the "wife who sacrifices all to nurse her helplessly invalid husband through endless tortuous years until death."[30] He goes on to say, however, that "unless she qualifies under some set of institutional rules, she may not be entitled" to a reward.[31] If she does not so qualify, it is hard to see how her being rewarded could be morally required. It is hard to see, in other words, how the deserts in such cases could be strictly normative.

Indeed, when rewards are deserved outside of institutional contexts, they probably belong not in Feinberg's third category, but in his fourth, as another informal response, and the deserts in category 4 clearly are not strictly normative. As we noted at the beginning of this section, the fact that someone deserves praise or blame implies nothing about requirements in others to praise or blame him, and the same is true for any other deserts that might belong in this category—deserts of credit or criticism, for example.

Perhaps there are types of deserved treatments that do not appear on Feinberg's list and that clearly exemplify strictly normative deserts. We will search no further for them here, however, resting content with the case we have constructed against the existence of such deserts. This case is certainly strong enough to cast serious doubt on the possibility of justifying R—and hence retributivism—by appealing to claims about the nature of desert alone.[32]

Summary

When people are legally punished, they are typically treated in ways that infringe rights in normal circumstances. The questions therefore arise as to whether punishment infringes the rights of those who are punished and, if so, whether the infringements are morally permissible. All versions of the no-infringement view incorporate the idea that the rights of wrongdoers are *not* infringed when the wrongdoers are punished. In contrast, theories falling within the permissible-infringement view are alike in implying that rights *are* infringed when people are punished, and they contain explanations of why infringing the rights of wrongdoers is permissible.

The most common forms of the no-infringement view are those based on the idea that people forfeit certain of their rights when they engage in wrongdoing, so that there are no rights to infringe when wrongdoers are punished. Although familiar deterrence and retributivist theories can be interpreted as falling within the no-infringement view, they are better construed as versions of the permissible-infringement view. The same is true of the account developed later in this book of punishment as societal-defense. Theories of punishment based on the idea of a societal right to punish are typically found within the no-infringement view but can profitably be examined as versions of the permissible-infringement view as well.

According to deterrence theories, considerations of deterrence are necessarily relevant to whether punishment is justified. Depending on the type of deterrence theory, considerations of deterrence are interpreted as capable of functioning in one or the other of two ways: as conditions that are sufficient for punishment to be required or as considerations that can defeat moral presumptions against punishment. Deterrence theories therefore imply that, if punishment effectively deters wrongdoing, then it is at least presumptively required.

Deterrence theories are of various sorts. In particular, some imply that forward-looking considerations are the only ones necessarily relevant to whether punishment is justified, while others imply that such considerations are only among those necessarily relevant to the justifiability of punishment. Moreover, theories in both groups can be either single-level or double-level. That is, they can focus exclusively on the justifiability of particular acts of punishment, or they can be concerned not only with individual punishments, but also with systems of punishment.

The most familiar deterrence theories of punishment are versions of act utilitarianism for punishment. Such theories have well-known defects, among the most prominent of which is their inability to accommodate the necessary relevance of considerations of guilt and innocence to whether acts of punishment are justified. Rule utilitarianism for punishment, which is seen by its proponents as free from this defect, is in fact objectionable on analogous grounds. That is, rule utilitarianism for punishment cannot accommodate the necessary relevance of general considerations of guilt and innocence to whether systems of punishment are justified.

Although retributivism is characterized differently by different writers, one important form is desert based in the sense that it centers on these propositions: punishments are required on the basis of their being deserved; and forms of punishment must correspond appropriately to types of wrongdoings. Assuming that the retributivist requirement to punish wrongdoers is presumptive, it follows that considerations of desert must be capable of prescriptively defeating moral presumptions against punishment. If claims about the nature of desert are basic components of retributivism, then considerations of desert must be capable of defeating moral presumptions in contexts having nothing to do with punishment. That is, there must be situations unrelated to punishment in which people are presumptively required to treat others in certain ways simply because the latter deserve to be treated in those ways. On examining contexts in which deserts appear to function in this manner, however, we find that the defeating considerations present in these contexts are not deserts at all. They are either special obligations arising from certain actions performed by those who are obligated, or they are institutional obligations. These results cast considerable doubt on the acceptability of desert-based retributivism.

Chapter 2

Defending and Preserving Individuals

Punishment and Self-Defense

In this chapter we begin developing a particular version of the permissible-infringement view, namely, the societal-defense theory of punishment referred to above. As we noted, this theory centers on the concept of societal-defense, which is analogous in significant respects to the concept of individual self-defense.

Punishment as societal-defense is a version of the permissible-infringement view in that it embodies a proposal for defeasibility conditions for the presumption against punishment—a proposal that differs importantly from those contained in traditional accounts of the justification of punishment. The intuitive appeal—as well as the problematic character—of our approach is indicated in the following remarks by Stephen Nathanson regarding the morality of capital punishment.

> although killing is generally immoral, there are certain kinds of killings which are justifiable, and one of them is killing in self-defense or in defense of others. Executing a murderer is not itself a case of killing in self-defense, but if death penalty advocates could show that the practice of executing murderers strongly resembles defensive killings in morally relevant ways, that would be an argument for including it on our list of justifiable exceptions. . . .
>
> When we compare executions with defensive killings, however, a problem arises immediately. A key factor in our judgment that killing in defense of oneself or others is morally justified is that the victim's life is actually saved by killing the attacker. This crucial factor is missing, however, when the death penalty is inflicted, for the victim is already dead, and the execution of his murderer will not restore him to life.[1]

Nathanson's comments here are very much on the mark, although we shall see that the "problem" to which he refers can be avoided while

25

preserving important connections between the morality of self-defense
on the one hand, and the morality of punishment on the other. Another
aspect of Nathanson's comparison of punishment with self-defense is,
however, mistaken—or at least misleading.

Nathanson discusses the analogy between executions and self-defense killings in the course of examining what he calls "The Deterrence
Argument" for capital punishment. He characterizes this argument as
implying that

> [t]hough we are powerless to restore life to the dead through executing
> murderers, we can prevent other murders from occurring by imposing this
> punishment. The death penalty on this view, is a kind of social self-de-
> fense, an act which, like cases of individual self-defense, results in saving
> the lives of innocent persons.[2]

Nathanson seems to be suggesting that an account of capital punishment
(or of punishment in general, presumably) relying on morally relevant
similarities between punishment and self-defense would be a kind of
deterrence theory. However, while this sort of suggestion might be in-
nocuous if deterrence theories are interpreted very broadly, it is mistaken if deterrence theories are given their standard interpretations. In
order to see why this is so, however, we clearly must look more closely
at the morality of both self- and societal-defense and then contrast punishment as societal-defense to deterrence theories as they were characterized in the preceding chapter. We will begin with a consideration
of why self-defense situations are so intriguing from a philosophical
standpoint.

Thomson on Self-Defense

In a discussion of self-defense killings, Judith Jarvis Thomson describes a hypothetical case in which one person (Aggressor) means to
kill another (Victim) by running her down with a tank. We are to assume that Victim cannot escape Aggressor's threat, but that she does
have an antitank gun capable of destroying the tank, although not without killing Aggressor. Thomson then says of this case:

> I think that most people would say that it is morally permissible for Victim
> to use that anti-tank gun: surely it is permissible to kill a man if that is the
> only way in which you can prevent him from killing you!
> On the other hand, one of the things we are firmly wedded to is the

belief that human beings have a right to life, and this presumably includes the right to not be killed. Aggressor is a human being; so he, like the rest of us, has a right to life, and presumably, therefore, the right to not be killed. So how *can* Victim kill him? Precisely *why* is it permissible for Victim to use that anti-tank gun on Aggressor?[3]

According to Thomson, then, the philosophical problem of self-defense arises largely from the idea that everyone has a right not to be killed. She suggests that solving these problems requires explaining how, in the face of this right, it can be permissible to kill another person even if the killing is done in defense of one's own life.

Underlying this characterization of the problem of self-defense is the assumption that the right not to be killed is a *claim* right: the possession of that right by some individual implies corresponding obligations in others. Thus, if Aggressor has a right not to be killed, then Victim is obligated not to kill him. Then if we say, as it seems we must, that Victim is permitted to kill Aggressor, we seem forced to conclude that Aggressor has no right to not be killed—and hence no right to life. Thomson examines several grounds for denying or at least qualifying Aggressor's right to life, and she argues quite convincingly that all are seriously defective. She concludes by suggesting that a satisfactory resolution of the self-defense issue awaits "an account of just how an appeal to a right may be thought to function in ethical discussion."[4] Although Thomson is doubtless correct in emphasizing the role that an account of rights must play in any satisfactory theory of self-defense, such an account is but one piece of a rather complex puzzle. The nature of these complexities is worth examining further.

We begin by characterizing what we will call "standard self-defense situations." These are situations that satisfy the following conditions: (1) an individual X acts with the intention of killing individual Y; (2) if X is not prevented from doing so, he will in fact kill Y; (3) X's aggression is wrongful in the sense that, if X were to carry out his intention to kill Y, he would be culpable or blameworthy for causing Y's death; (4) Y and only Y is in a position to prevent X from carrying out his intention, and she can do so only by killing X; and (5) Y, who is aware of her plight, can kill X without killing anyone else. Next we suppose (following Thomson) that everyone, including aggressors in standard self-defense situations, has a right to life. We then imagine that, in Thomson's example, Victim fights back—she starts shooting at Aggressor.

Now, if we examine the conditions listed here in terms of which we characterized standard self-defense situations, we find that all save one can be satisfied by a situation in which Aggressor's life is threatened by Victim's defensive actions. Thus, we can certainly imagine a situation in which the following are true: Victim fights back with the intention of killing Aggressor, recognizing that only by killing Aggressor can she save her own life; if Victim is not prevented from doing so, she will kill Aggressor; Aggressor is the only one who can prevent himself from being killed by Victim, and he can do so only by killing Victim; and Aggressor can kill Victim without killing anyone else. The only reason that this situation is not a standard self-defense situation is that it fails to satisfy the condition that refers to wrongful aggression: while Aggressor's attack on Victim is impermissible, Victim is permitted to fight back.

Let us suppose that the situation described by Thomson meets the conditions listed above, and is therefore standard. Suppose too that Aggressor's killing of Victim would be impermissible by virtue of violating Victim's right to life, but that Victim's infringing Aggressor's right to life is permissible for some reason. There is then a clear sense in which their positions are morally asymmetrical relative to each other. Determining the moral dimensions of self-defense can thus be thought of as an asymmetry problem—that is, the problem of explaining *why* the positions of aggressors and of their intended victims in standard situations are asymmetrical in the manner just described.

How might this problem be solved? Perhaps by invoking the plausible idea that everyone has not only a right to life, but also a right of self-defense. Since Victim would be exercising this right if she killed Aggressor to save her own life, and since Aggressor is not exercising the right of self-defense when he initiates his attack, we seem to have an explanation of why Aggressor's position is morally asymmetrical with respect to Victim's. But suppose now that Victim fights back, and that she thereby poses a deadly threat to Aggressor. If everyone has a right of self-defense, then Aggressor has this right—from which it follows that Aggressor has a right to kill Victim in response to the latter's fighting back. In other words, it appears that in these latter circumstances both Aggressor and Victim are exercising the same right. If this is the case, then, just as Victim is permitted to kill Aggressor in defense of her life, so Aggressor is permitted to kill Victim when she fights back. Yet Victim's and Aggressor's situations are definitely not morally symmetrical in this way: Aggressor is not permitted to kill Victim in response to defensive actions on the latter's part. Hence, while we might solve the first asymmetry problem by appealing to the idea of a right of self-defense, such an appeal generates a second asymmetry problem—that of explaining why Victim is permitted to kill Aggressor in self-defense, while the latter is not permitted to kill Victim if she fights back.

Thomson has recently reexamined the morality of self-defense, and in the course of doing so she offers an explanation of why targets of deadly threats in situations of the sort she describes in her original example are permitted to kill in self-defense. Her more recent account also contains an explanation of why aggressors are not permitted to harm their intended victims when the latter fight back. Hence—unlike most other writers on the morality of self-defense—Thomson offers solutions to both of the asymmetry problems described above.

Thomson develops her account as part of a wider examination of various situations in which the actions of people endanger the lives of others. Although her broader discussion is illuminating and insightful, we needn't examine it right now. For the present we can focus exclusively on Thomson's explanation of why killing in self-defense is permissible in standard self-defense situations. To understand Thomson's account as it applies to these situations, it will be useful for us to expand her example so that it includes a period of time just prior to Aggressor's attack on Victim. We will assume that during this time both protagonists are minding their own business, posing no threats to anyone else. Thomson's account implies that under these conditions both Aggressor and Victim have rights against each other not to be killed. This is because, according to Thomson, "Other things being equal, every person Y has a right against X that X not kill Y,"[5] and in the circumstances we are presently imagining other things *are* equal insofar as they concern both Aggressor and Victim.

Moreover, other things remain equal insofar as they concern Victim when Aggressor launches his attack, so that Victim continues to have a right not to be killed by Aggressor. The following propositions are therefore true of Thomson's example: if Aggressor kills Victim, then he will infringe or violate her right not to be killed by him, and the only way for Victim to avoid being killed by Aggressor is to kill him. According to Thomson, these two propositions imply that other things are *not* equal insofar as they concern Aggressor. Thomson concludes from this line of reasoning that Aggressor has no right not to be killed by Victim and that Victim's killing Aggressor is therefore morally permissible.

A more precise formulation of this argument again begins with the principle that

(1) Other things being equal, every person Y has a right against [every other person X] that X not kill Y.

We then say that the *ceteris paribus* condition contained in this principle is satisfied for victims in standard situations. In terms of Thomson's example, then, we have

(2) Other things are equal insofar as they concern Victim.

And (1) and (2) are to be understood as entailing

(3) Victim has a right against Aggressor that Aggressor not kill Victim.

The next component of Thomson's argument is the claim that the *ceteris paribus* condition in (1) is not satisfied for aggressors in standard cases, which implies that

(4) Other things are not equal insofar as they concern Aggressor,

and (4) is claimed by Thomson to follow from the conjunction of (3) with "the only way Victim can avoid being killed by Aggressor is by killing Aggressor." The next step in the argument is to reason from (1) and (4) to

(5) Aggressor does not have a right against Victim that Victim not kill Aggressor.

The argument's final step consists in reasoning from (5) to "Victim is permitted to kill Aggressor."

If Thomson's account worked, then it would solve the first asymmetry problem: it would explain why victims are permitted to kill aggressors but aggressors are not permitted to kill victims in standard situations. Moreover, it would do so in a wonderfully economical way. Additionally, it would furnish a partial solution to the second asymmetry problem, in that it would begin to explain why aggressors in standard situations are not permitted to kill their intended victims when the latter fight back against the formers' initial aggression, because since other things remain equal for victims when they fight back against aggressors (so that they retain their right not to be killed when they fight back), other things remain unequal for aggressors (so that they still have no right not to be killed by their intended victims).

By itself, however, this last conclusion would not completely solve the second asymmetry problem to which standard self-defense situations give rise. That is, it would not explain why—if everyone has a right of self-defense—aggressors in standard situations are not permitted to exercise this right in defending themselves against the defensive actions of their intended victims. An explanation of the requisite sort does seem implicit in Thomson's account, however. For if the proposition that people have a right not to be killed must be understood as containing an implicit *ceteris paribus* condition, then so presumably must the proposition that people have a right of self-defense. Presumably, too, the condition implicit in this latter proposition is not satisfied insofar as it concerns aggressors in standard self-defense situations. So if Thomson's account succeeds, then it explains both respects in which moral asymmetries obtain between aggressors and their intended victims in standard self-defense situations.

If the argument stated above is indeed Thomson's, however, then her account does not succeed, and this because the argument is fallacious. To see where the problem lies, we must look more closely at statements (1) through (5).

The natural interpretation for (1)—and an interpretation under which its conjunction with (2) entails (3)—is

(6) If other things are equal, then every person Y has a right against [every other person] X that X not kill Y.

But if (1) is equated with (6), then it no longer entails (5) when conjoined with (4). Of course, the conjunction of (1) with (4) does entail (5) if (1) is interpreted as equivalent to

(7) Every person Y has a right against [every other person X] that X not kill Y only if other things are equal.

But if (1) is equated with (7), then it no longer entails (3) when conjoined with (2); and (3) is not only essential in itself to Thomson's position, but it is also required to infer (4).

While it might not be entirely clear from Thomson's discussion how she interprets (1), not only does most of what she says suggest that she regards it as equivalent to (6), but (6) is also a much more plausible translation of (1) than (7) is. How this issue should be resolved is irrelevant to the point being made here, however. For regardless of whether Thomson interprets (1) according to (6) or according to (7), her central argument is invalid, and her explanation of why self-defense is permissible in standard situations must be rejected.

Thomson's invalid argument could be converted to one that is valid by abandoning (1) in favor of something like, "Every person Y has a right against X that X not kill Y *if and only if* other things are equal." While the resulting argument would be valid, however, its new premise—and hence its soundness—would be open to serious question. We noted above that great difficulties are involved in filling the blanks in expressions such as, "One has a right not to receive treatment that is K only if . . . ," and similar difficulties would certainly also arise in connection with propositions of the form, "One has a right not to receive treatment that is K provided that. . . ." The difficulties associated with these propositions, while very serious, are almost certainly less serious than those associated with producing conditions that are both necessary and sufficient for people to possess the right not to be killed.

The difficulties afflicting Thomson's account are quite obviously connected with her view of how principles about rights should be formulated. Interestingly enough, her "other things being equal" formulation is a version of a view whose two other versions she rejects in her first discussion of self-defense. She characterizes these latter views, as well as the general view of which they are versions, in this passage.

> I mean to use the term "specification" so as to cover two connected replies [to the question of why Victim's killing Aggressor is permissible]. Both begin in the same way. "You only think there's a problem here because you think that 'Aggressor has a right to life' entails 'Aggressor has a right to not be killed.' But it doesn't. We all do have a right to life, but that right to life is a more complicated business than it at first may appear to be. In particular, having a right to life *doesn't* include having a right to not be killed. Indeed, *nobody* has a right to not be killed: all you have is—" and here there are two ways in which the speaker may go on. I will call the first "moral specification": ". . . all you have is the right to not be wrongly, unjustly killed." I will call the second "factual specification": ". . . all you have is the right to not be killed if you are not in process of trying to kill a person, where that person has every reason to believe he can preserve his life only by killing you."[6]

Thomson then offers compelling arguments against each form of specification. More to the point here, however, is her claim that both forms of specification suffer from an additional, common defect, namely, that they both presuppose "an incorrect view of rights . . . that rights are, in a certain sense, *absolute*."[7] Given Thomson's characterizations of factual and moral specification, there is reason to suppose that her "other things being equal" view of rights is also a form of specification—perhaps even a form of factual or moral specification.

There is also reason to believe that the absolutist view of rights that Thomson claims is incorrect is presupposed by her own account, as well as by the two forms of specification that she criticizes, for all three accounts interpret principles affirming the existence of rights as containing implicit provisos of one sort or another. This interpretation of such principles is clearly evident in Thomson's later discussion, where her principle, "Other things being equal, every person Y has a right against X that X not kill Y" is evidently equivalent to "Every person Y has a right against X that X not kill Y provided that other things are equal." The more basic similarity between Thomson's view and specification of the two types she discusses is that both presuppose that inferences from principles affirming the existence of rights (e.g., "Everyone has a right to not be killed") to propositions attributing rights to particular individuals (e.g., "You have a right to not be killed here and now") are deductive.

An additional difficulty with Thomson's view is worth mentioning, because it is one that plagues all attempts to justify homicide in self-defense on the basis of claims about the existence of conditions necessary for individuals to possess a right to life. Thus, suppose we agree with Thomson that one has a right to life only if she is not culpably threatening the life of an innocent person. Then a sufficient condition for someone to lack a right to life—an "alienation condition" for that right—is that she is a culpable aggressor in a standard self-defense situation. But suppose that someone were to insist that only the actual and culpable infliction of serious harm on others—perhaps only murder—is bad enough to result in alienation of the right to life. This view (espoused by many defenders of capital punishment) is at least as plausible as Thomson's. How are we to know which, if either, of these views is correct? More important, on what principled basis does one determine the alienation conditions for specific rights? Thomson does not address this question. Yet, in the absence of a basis of the requisite sort, there is no reason at all to accept claims like Thomson's about the alienation conditions for some particular right.

Thomson is not, of course, the only writer to have examined problems associated with self-defense, but her examination differs from almost all others in three respects that explain why it is the only one we will examine here: first, it is characteristically thorough and seems (at least initially) to be quite plausible; second, it focuses on the moral rather than the legal dimensions of self-defense; and, third, it offers solutions to both of the asymmetry problems that are generated by standard self-defense situations. Having found Thomson's account wanting, we will now develop an alternative explanation of the morality of self-defense and an alternative proposal for solving the asymmetry problems to which standard self-defense situations give rise.[8]

Forced Choices

In standard self-defense situations people are permitted to kill others in defense of their own lives. Such situations, however, are not the only ones in which people are permitted to kill (or otherwise to cause the deaths of) others to save themselves. Such acts are sometimes permissible in nonstandard self-defense situations, as well as under conditions having nothing to do with *defending* one's own life from aggressive or otherwise threatening behavior on the part of others.

Consider, for example, the following variation on the "runaway trolley" theme. A runaway trolley, with no operator and with Al as its sole passenger, is approaching a fork in the tracks; if nothing is done, the car will continue forward and over a steep cliff and Al certainly will be killed. Al can turn the car onto a siding, but if he does, he will run over and kill someone stuck in the tracks. It seems quite clear that, other things being equal, Al is permitted to maneuver the trolley so that he saves himself, even though another person will die as a result, and even though Al is not acting in self-defense. One is also permitted, and sometimes required, to kill in defense of others and even to save their lives when not, strictly speaking, defending them. That there are cases of the former sort is quite obvious; that the latter also exist is more controversial, although plain enough. We need only modify our original example, so that Al is faced with the choice of doing nothing and allowing the car to run over and kill someone stuck in the tracks ahead, or of turning onto a siding with the result that someone else is killed. Diehard defenders of the distinction between killing and letting-die might insist that Al is not under any circumstances permitted to turn the car, but while we will not argue the point, this kind of claim does seem mistaken.

All these cases, as well as some others we will consider presently, have a feature that we will find is of considerable importance for our inquiry: they all involve "forced choices" among lives. The sense in which we are thinking of choices as forced needs some clarification, however. It is especially important to emphasize that forced choices are not necessarily compelled or coerced choices. A choice's being forced (in the relevant sense) is completely compatible with its being free or responsible and is a proper object of moral appraisal.[9] To say that someone faces a forced choice between lives is for our purposes simply to say that, regardless of what the person does, at least one of the lives will be lost, although the person is in a position to determine *which* life is (lives are) lost. Let us say that the lives at stake in a forced choice situation comprise the ''field'' of that choice.

Given that, in addition to standard self-defense situations, there is a variety of other situations in which people are permitted to choose in their own favor when faced with forced choices between their own lives and those of others, what are the moral similarities and differences between these situations? Descriptions of various forced-choice situations will aid us in our attempt to answer this question.

Earlier, we characterized standard self-defense situations as those that satisfy the following conditions: (1) an individual X acts with the intention of killing individual Y; (2) if X is not prevented from doing so, he will in fact kill Y; (3) X's aggression is wrongful in the sense that, if X were to carry out his intention to kill Y, Y's death would be X's fault; (4) Y and only Y is in a position to prevent X from carrying out his intention, and she can do so only by killing X; and (5) Y (who is aware of her plight) can kill X without killing anyone else. In situations satisfying these conditions choices among lives are forced in the sense explained above, but choices among lives can also be forced in situations that fail to satisfy one or more of conditions (1) through (5). They include nonstandard self-defense cases of the following kinds.

(D1)   Aggression is involved, but the aggression is not wrongful, since those engaged in the aggression are not responsible for their actions. For example, they might be suffering from certain kinds of mental disorders (''innocent aggressor'' cases).

(D2)   The only way for a target of wrongful aggression to save his own life is by killing not only the aggressor, but also some number of innocent bystanders (''innocent bystander'' cases).

Note that, in standard situations as well as in D2 cases, there are moral asymmetries among at least some of the individuals comprising the fields of the forced choices in those cases. We have already discussed the asymmetries that obtain between aggressors and their intended victims in standard situations, and these same asymmetries are present in D2 cases—but only between the aggressors and victims in those cases. There is no moral asymmetry between targets of wrongful aggression and innocent bystanders in D2 cases. And, as we shall now argue, since all those comprising the fields of the forced choices in D1 cases are innocent, their positions are morally symmetrical with respect to each other.

Moral symmetries and asymmetries being distributed in D1 and D2 cases in the manner just suggested receives support from a consideration of the idea of fighting back that we employed in examining the moral asymmetry between victims and aggressors in standard situations. That is, we imagine the targets of aggression in D1 and D2 cases as fighting back and consider whether innocent aggressors and innocent bystanders are then permitted to act in defense of their own lives by killing those against whom their initial attacks are directed. It seems that they are and that their positions therefore differ in morally significant ways from the wrongful aggressors in both standard situations and D2 cases, where fighting back against the defensive measures of their intended victims is morally impermissible.

The idea that innocent bystanders and innocent aggressors are morally on a par is by no means self-evident and might well be rejected by some.[10] After all, it might be argued, homicidal maniacs would seem to be innocent in the relevant sense, and yet their moral status vis-à-vis their innocent victims is certainly different from the moral status of innocent bystanders vis-à-vis the intended victims in D2 cases.

This objection, however, seems to presuppose—mistakenly—that anyone whose aggression stems from serious mental abnormalities automatically qualifies as an innocent aggressor. Without attempting to characterize the mental abnormalities that produce innocence, clear examples of aggression that is innocent in the relevant sense are easy to construct. Thus, through no fault of her own, someone might suffer a hallucination that convinces her that some other person is about to kill her, causing her to attempt to kill the latter in "self-defense." That this person is innocent in the relevant sense can be seen by comparing her situation vis-à-vis her "intended victim" with that of a person who aims a loaded gun at someone else, intending to shoot her, and who does so in the mistaken but justified belief that he is in imminent danger of being murdered by her. Surely the person aiming the gun is an innocent aggressor in the relevant sense of "innocent," and if he is, then so is our imaginary hallucinator. The point is that the difference between being an aggressor and being a bystander is not in and of itself morally significant.

Self-defense situations (whether standard or nonstandard) can be distinguished from what we will call "self-preservation" situations. In the latter an individual is forced to choose between his own life and that of others, but none of the others are aggressors. The following kinds of cases exemplify self-preservation situations.

(P1) No one acts with the intention of causing another's death, but a deadly threat is posed by someone's culpable recklessness or negligence.

(P2) Someone's life is in danger as a result of someone else's actions, but the threat arises completely by accident and with no contributory recklessness or negligence on anyone's part ("accidental threat" cases).

(P3) A target of culpable aggression can save his own life without killing the aggressor, but not without killing some innocent person. ("innocent threat" cases).

(P4) Through no one's fault, circumstances arise in which someone must choose between his life and that of an innocent person, where the latter is not doing anything that poses a threat to the former ("pure self-preservation" cases).[11]

Some specific examples of our first three kinds of self-preservation situations will be useful. (We already have an example of P4 situations in the first of our two runaway trolley cases.)

Here is a P1 case involving culpable negligence: You are invited to go sailing by an acquaintance (Bo) who is himself a highly experienced and skilled sailor. You never have been sailing before and must therefore rely completely on Bo to plan and prepare for the trip. The two of you set off one morning and by that afternoon you are many miles from shore. Suddenly, you are hit by a severe storm that so damages the boat that it begins sinking and, in the process, knocks Bo unconscious. Bo knew that a storm was on its way before he set sail, but he ignored the danger out of extreme self-confidence. He also failed to provide an additional life vest after noticing that there was only one on board. You are now faced with the choice of donning the life vest, and thereby saving your life but allowing Bo to drown, or putting the vest on Bo with the result that his life is saved but you drown.

The following is a P2 (accidental threat) case: Cal, who drives a very large truck carrying gravel, is about to dump his load into a ditch. He is unaware (and cannot reasonably be expected to be aware) that you have fallen into the ditch and cannot extricate yourself before he dumps his load. The only way for you to prevent yourself from being killed by Cal is to destroy his truck, with the result that Cal will be killed.

The following P3 (innocent threat) case is borrowed from Robert Nozick:[12] You are trapped at the bottom of a deep well with no room at all to maneuver. Dot is peering down at you, trying to think of a way to bring you up, when she is pushed in by Ed. If Dot lands on you, you will be killed but she will be unharmed. You do have a ray gun, though, and you can save your own life by firing at Dot, causing her to be atomized.

As we did in discussing the three types of self-defense cases characterized above, we can consider possible moral asymmetries among the people who comprise the fields of the forced choices in our four types of self-preservation cases. Since all the individuals in the fields of the forced choices in P2, P3, and P4 cases are innocent, there are no moral asymmetries among them.[13] Those whose lives are endangered in such cases are permitted to opt in favor of self-preservation even though their doing so would result in the deaths of other innocent people, and the permissibility of choosing in one's own favor extends to those whose lives become threatened by acts of self-preservation on the part of others.

Thus, for example, consider again our accidental threat case in which your life is endangered when Cal begins to dump his load of gravel into the ditch you occupy. You are permitted to destroy the truck and kill Cal in defense of your life, but, assuming Cal has a gun, he is permitted to defend his life by firing at you in defense of his life. Similarly, Dot is permitted to use her own ray gun in defense of her life even if you would be killed as a result; and, if the person stuck in the tracks whose life is threatened when Al turns the car starts shooting at Al, Al is permitted to shoot back.

In contrast to these P2, P3, and P4 cases, however, asymmetries are present in P1 cases. We can see this by comparing our original sailing example with a case in which you are the unconscious person, and Bo is faced with the decision whether to buckle you into the life vest or to use it himself. It seems clear that, because Bo is to blame for your predicament, his using the vest himself would be morally impermissible, while your using it in our original example would be morally permissible.

Let us now add to our list ''other-defense'' and ''other-preservation'' situations analogous to the self-defense and self-preservation cases just described. For example, standard other-defense situations are exactly like standard self-defense situations except that in place of condition (4) we have (4'): Z and only Z is in a position to prevent X from carrying out his intention to kill Y, and the only way Z can do so is by killing

X; and in place of (5) we have (5′): Z can kill X without killing anyone else.

The moral symmetries and asymmetries present in other-defense and other-preservation situations exactly parallel those present in the corresponding self-defense and self-preservation situations; and the former symmetries and asymmetries have significant moral implications for third-party actions and refrainings. In standard other-defense situations, for example, third parties in positions to do so are morally required to act in defense of targets of aggression in those cases; whereas they are only permitted to act in defense of targets of aggression in innocent aggressor cases. More generally, if members of the field of a forced choice are morally symmetrical with respect to each other, then third parties are permitted to defend or preserve any of their lives. But when asymmetries obtain among members of the field of a forced choice, third parties are morally required to defend or preserve the lives of those who are permitted to defend or preserve their own lives.

Moreover, there is an important sense in which numbers count when making forced choices among morally symmetrical lives but are irrelevant in the presence of moral asymmetries. That is, the asymmetries present in standard self- and other-defense situations, and in P1 cases and their third-party correlates, extend to situations in which one person's life is threatened by the culpably aggressive, negligent, or reckless acts of *many* other people. However, the symmetries obtaining among those belonging to the fields of the forced choices in D1, P2, P3, and P4 cases and in their third-party correlates do not extend to situations that involve many innocent aggressors, bystanders, or threats. Thus, for example, targets of aggression in standard self-defense situations are permitted to kill as many wrongful aggressors as is necessary to save their own lives, and parallel remarks apply to requirements for third parties in standard other-defense situations. Targets of aggression in D1 situations, however, are not permitted to kill many innocent aggressors to save their own lives, and parallel remarks apply to third parties in the other-defense correlates of such situations.

Underlying the claims just made is a line of thinking that goes like this: When faced with a forced choice among lives, it is sometimes permissible to cause the deaths of some number of persons in order to save the lives of others. The fact that one course of action in a forced choice situation involves *defending* someone's life from someone else's aggressive or threatening behavior is one among many factors relevant to whether causing someone's death is permissible, but does not in itself distinguish, from a moral standpoint, defensive forced choice situations from others in which causing the deaths of people is permissible. Special moral significance does attach, however, to the fact that a life-threatening situation is created by someone's *culpable* behavior, whether intentional, reckless, or negligent. We can put this point another way. If moral symmetries obtain among those comprising the fields of the forced choices in defense or preservation cases, whether "self" or "other," then these cases are all in very much the same moral boat. These cases differ significantly, however, from defense or preservation cases that involve moral asymmetries among members of the fields of their forced choices.

Forced Choices and the Distribution of Burdens

Our next task is to provide a principled basis for the claims made in the preceding section regarding the similarities and differences that exist among the types of self- and other-defense cases and the types of self- and other-preservation cases we have discussed. There is a passage in Locke's *Second Treatise* that is worth examining in this regard, particularly with respect to questions about self-defense situations involving culpably aggressive behavior. After he discusses the state of nature and its laws and their relation to government and its laws, Locke explains the state of war.

> The state of war is a state of enmity and destruction; and therefore declaring by word or action, not a passionate and hasty, but a sedate, settled design upon another man's life, puts him in a state of war with him against whom he has declared such an intention, and so has exposed his life to the other's power to be taken away by him, or anyone that joins with him in his defence and espouses his quarrel; it being reasonable and just I should have a right to destroy that which threatens me with destruction. For by the fundamental law of nature, man being to be preserved as much as possible, when all cannot be preserved, the safety of the innocent is to be preferred; and one may destroy a man who makes war upon him, or has discovered an enmity to his being, for the same reason that he may kill a wolf or a lion; because they are not under the ties of the common law of reason, have no other rule but that of force and violence, and so may be treated as a beast of prey, those dangerous and noxious creatures that will be sure to destroy him whenever he falls into their power.[14]

Without worrying too much about what precisely Locke has in mind here, it is possible to discern in this passage at least two independent, although not mutually exclusive, approaches to standard self-defense situations. On the one hand there is the idea that the requirements of morality, or at least those concerned with killing, are reciprocal: they oblige us to behave or to refrain from behaving in certain ways toward others just as long as those others remain within the bounds of civility. On the other hand there is the idea that those who intentionally and cold-bloodedly try to kill others devalue themselves or, perhaps, their interests to the point that killing them is of little or no moral consequence. It seems doubtful that an adequate philosophical account of self-defense can be based on either of these ideas in themselves, although both contain a measure of plausibility, and traces of one or the other are commonly present in both philosophical and legal discussions of self-defense.[15]

Combining Locke's two ideas, we have something like this: that one individual's obligation to refrain from killing another is reciprocal in the sense of becoming less stringent if the other attempts to kill the given individual. The plausibility of this combined idea increases if it is located in a more general context. Accordingly, let us broaden our scope somewhat to include cases in which no one's life is at stake but in which the stringency of one person's obligation to another does seem dependent on the other's behavior. Thus, consider the following example: you have promised an acquaintance that you will teach her to drive; in the course of your lessons, your acquaintance becomes obnoxious and insulting to you, despite the fact that you are a good and conscientious teacher. It seems obvious that, in the face of your acquaintance's churlish behavior, you are permitted to end the lessons, your promise notwithstanding.

If we were to apply this line of thinking to standard self-defense situations, then we would presumably say that aggressors in those situations act in ways that weaken their intended victims' obligations not to kill the aggressors. Identifying the relevant actions performed by aggressors is no easy matter, however, and explaining why they affect the obligations of intended victims is even more difficult. The obvious candidate for the type of actions in question—acts of aggression aimed at killing another—will not do without some way of excluding acts of fighting back on the part of victims, and it is very hard to see how to exclude these latter acts in a way that does not beg the question at hand.

To resolve these issues it will be helpful to examine a third idea that is present in the Locke quotation—an idea that is easily overlooked because it appears at first glance not to cut very deeply. Locke states that "... by the fundamental law of nature, man being to be preserved as much as possible, when all cannot be preserved, the safety of the innocent is to be preferred . . .'' In standard self-defense situations, ''the innocent'' would presumably be those who are the intended victims of wrongful aggression; and their safety is to be given preference over that of those engaged in such aggression. While Locke goes on to suggest that the former should be favored because the latter are like ''beasts of prey,'' this choice can be based on a rather different and more plausible consideration.

This consideration is best explained by again broadening the scope of our discussion and considering a class of cases that satisfy the following conditions: (1) the members of a certain group of people are situated so that, from the standpoint of an individual X (who is not necessarily included in the group), harm will unavoidably befall some but not all of them; (2) that they are so situated is the fault of some but not all members of the groups (and is not X's fault); and (3) X is in a position to determine who will be harmed. In cases satisfying these conditions X is faced with a forced choice among harms: harm is unavoidable from X's standpoint, although X is in a position to distribute the harm in various ways. It is certainly plausible to say that, if X does not belong to the endangered group, he is required, as a matter of basic justice in the distribution of burdens, to distribute the harm so that it befalls those whose fault it is that there is harm to be distributed. If, however, X is part of the threatened group but is in no way responsible for their predicament, then he is not required to distribute the harm in a manner that favors himself over the guilty parties, but he is permitted to do so.

The ''matter of basic justice in the distribution of burdens'' to which we have referred can be put in the form of a principle that applies to standard self-defense situations and to the broader class of cases described in (1) through (4) above to which standard situations belong.

(J) When members of a group of individuals are in danger of being harmed through the fault of some, but not all, members of that group; and when some person (who might but need not be a member of the endangered group and who is in any case not at fault) is in a position to determine how the harm is distributed, even though the harm is unavoidable from that person's standpoint; then the person has a right (if a member of the threatened group) and is required (if not a member of the group) to distribute the harm among those who are at fault.[16]

It is not hard to see how J applies to standard self-defense situations such as that depicted by Thomson. Victim is faced with a forced choice between Aggressor's life and her own, and it is Aggressor's fault that Victim must make this choice between lives. Victim therefore has a right to choose in her own favor, and an appropriately situated third party would be required to act in Victim's defense. Moreover, justice permits this same choice of Victim, and would require it of a third-party, no matter how many wrongful aggressors must be killed to save Victim.

Analogous statements apply to P1 cases—self-preservation cases involving culpable recklessness or negligence—such as our example of your sailing trip with Bo. It is Bo's fault that you are forced to choose between your life and his (the situations having been brought about by his culpable negligence), and, hence, according to the line of reasoning developed above, you are permitted, and an appropriately situated third party would be required, to choose your life over his. Moreover, you would still be permitted to choose in your own favor if the case were modified along these lines: Bo and his expert crew are all culpably negligent in causing your predicament, and you, or a third-party, are forced to choose between your one life and the many lives of Bo and his crew.

Clearly, then, J applies to the cases of interest to us here. But is it in fact an acceptable principle? We will address this question below, but first some clarification of J is called for. We will begin by considering the idea that J is a principle of distributive justice, although we will return to this topic in the next chapter.

That J is a principle of distributive justice might be overlooked, given the common tendency in discussions of justice to focus exclusively on the distribution of *benefits*. Clearly, situations can arise in which there are burdens to distribute. In some of these situations the burdens are unavoidable from the standpoints of those in positions to distribute them, so that the latter face forced choices regarding their distribution. That is, situations can arise in which, no matter what is done by some individual, someone will be burdened—although the former has options regarding how the burdens are distributed. When such situations arise, it is natural to look for reasonable criteria on the basis of which to determine which distributions are most just.

Because cases of self-defense, self-preservation, and so on, are not normally thought of as providing contexts within which principles of distributive justice are applicable, let us consider an example to which J applies and with respect to which appealing to distributive justice is quite natural.

Though culpable negligence on her part, the owner of a chemical factory has allowed highly toxic materials to escape through the factory's smokestacks. These materials are blown into some neighboring fields, killing the cows grazing there. As a result, the rancher who owns the cows suffers a substantial financial loss and petitions Absolute Ruler for recovery of damages. Absolute Ruler has three options at her disposal: she can do nothing, leaving the rancher with his loss; she can require the factory owner to compensate the rancher for his dead cows; or she can cover the rancher's loss with funds paid in taxes by her subjects.

Absolute Ruler is here faced with a situation in which there are burdens to be distributed, and the burdens are unavoidable from her standpoint. Which of the three available distributions does justice require? Surely, the one in which the factory owner compensates the rancher: after all, it is her fault that there are unavoidable burdens to be distributed, so she rather than the rancher or the general populace should bear those burdens. This distribution is exactly the one required by J.[17]

Now consider the following example to which J applies under certain assumptions, but to which it does not apply under others.

The public resources available for medical treatment in society S are insufficient to meet all the needs of the members of S. If no public resources are provided for persons whose illnesses are due to their smoking, however, then all other medical needs can be met. Everyone in S has personal resources sufficient to meet his or her medical needs, but for everyone the lack of public assistance would result in considerable hardship.

Suppose now that Absolute Ruler controls the distribution of public funds for the medical needs of members of S. Suppose also that every member of S who smokes began voluntarily and continues voluntarily, that all smokers know that their smoking places them at high risk of becoming seriously ill, and that it is their fault that they are ill as a result of smoking. Suppose finally that no other members of S who require medical treatment are in any way at fault for being ill.

While Absolute Ruler can be thought of as being in a position to distribute benefits (i.e., funds for medical treatment), she can also be seen as responsible for distributing burdens (i.e., sacrifices required to meet medical needs without public assistance). On this latter interpretation, moreover, the burdens that Absolute Ruler is responsible for distributing are unavoidable from her standpoint, so that she is faced with a forced choice in the distribution of those burdens. Since it is the fault of certain potential recipients of the burdens that there are burdens to be distributed, J (presumptively) requires Absolute Ruler to distribute the burdens in a way which favors those in S who are not ill as a result of smoking. If, however, we made no assumptions about fault on the smokers' part, then J would not apply to the case, and some other distribution principle would have to be appealed to in deciding how justly to distribute the available medical resources—or the sacrifices required by the lack of such resources—among the members of S.

Examining cases to which J applies and contrasting them to cases to which it does not apply help reveal not only what J is, but also what it is not. It is not, as some writers seem to suggest, a manifestation of the idea that, because choices are forced in certain situations involving the distribution of burdens, responsibility for those choices is removed from those who make them and relocated in those whose fault it is that there are burdens to be distributed.[18] The point here can most clearly be made in the context of standard self-defense situations.

Thus, suppose that, in Thomson's example, Victim kills Aggressor. One might think that, if J applies to this situation in the manner intended, then this is because—given Victim's forced choice—she is not responsible for Aggressor's death; and that, instead, Aggressor is responsible for his own death. But J presupposes no such shifts in responsibility. As was pointed out earlier, the relevant sense in which choices are forced has nothing to do with their being compelled or coerced. We can assume that Victim is responsible for Aggressor's death if she kills him in self-defense (i.e., causally responsible, but not morally responsible in the sense of being blameworthy), and still conclude from J that she did something morally permissible. There is, after all, no need to assume in our dead cow example that, if Absolute Ruler were to require the factory owner to compensate the rancher, she would not be responsible for doing so—that, instead, the factory owner herself is responsible for her having to pay compensation. The reasoning behind our conclusion in this case is no different from that behind our conclusions in standard self-defense situations.

As is the case with moral principles in general, J must be understood as defeasible, and three major defeasibility conditions for J are worth mentioning at this point. The first is a proportionality condition, according to which the distribution of unavoidable harm among those who are to blame for the existence of that harm must be proportional to the harm that would be suffered by innocent persons under a different distribution. It is important to recognize that this condition concerns individual rather than collective harm. If a choice must be made between distributing harm to one person or to several and if the several are jointly to blame for the existence of that harm, then the innocent person must be favored even if the total harm resulting from such a distribution is much greater than that which would result from a distribution favoring those who are culpable. According to the proportionality condition, however, the harm suffered by each blameworthy individual under a given distribution must be proportional to that which would be suffered by an innocent person under a different distribution.

Returning to our example of your sailing trip with Bo, the proportionality condition would prevent J from being used to justify doing major harm to Bo, or to any number of collectively culpable crew members, in order to save yourself from suffering minor harm. If the only harm possible in a given situation is the loss of life, then the proportionality condition is automatically satisfied and questions about the quantity of harm done do not arise unless innocent persons are affected differently by different distributions.

The proportionality condition places a maximum on the amount of unavoidable harm that may be done to individuals according to J. There is also a minimization condition, according to which those to blame for the existence of unavoidable harm may not themselves be harmed more than is necessary in order to protect innocent persons. Turning again to our sailing example, J with this minimization condition cannot be used to justify a distribution of harm that results in Bo's death if another distribution is possible that, although somewhat harmful to Bo, preserves his life as well as yours.

A third defeating condition for the presumption carried by J concerns the harmful side effects for innocent persons that might result from distributions of harm aimed at protecting other innocent persons. The need for this condition can be illustrated by innocent bystander cases. For example, we might have an other-defense version of Thomson's case in which a third party can save Victim's life by killing Aggressor, but if he does, then some innocent bystander will also be killed; while if the third party does not act in Victim's defense, the bystander will not be killed. Under these conditions J does not straightforwardly imply that the third party should defend Victim.

With these clarifying comments in mind, let us return to the question, raised above, of whether J is an acceptable moral principle. If—as has been claimed here—J embodies a requirement of *basic* justice, then its acceptability cannot be demonstrated by deriving it from some more fundamental principle. We will therefore proceed indirectly, by characterizing some intuitions that support J, by disposing of some potential counterexamples, and, in the next chapter by indicating how certain other principles of justice are inapplicable to the situations to which J applies. Our goal will be to create a presumptive case in favor of J, placing the burden of proof on those who would dispute its acceptability.

Note first of all that, although J might not be a very familiar principle, it embodies ideas that play significant roles in much commonsense thinking about the nature of justice. It is no doubt related to the very general principle that the good and bad things that happen to people should have some reasonably direct connection with their responsible behavior. According to a strong version of this principle, good things should befall those who behave well and bad things those who behave badly. According to a somewhat weaker version, good people should benefit if anyone does, and, if harm is unavoidable, then (*ceteris paribus*) the guilty rather than the innocent should suffer. J also embodies a sense of "cosmic justice" that leads us to think it unjust when good people suffer natural catastrophes and the wicked lead carefree and happy lives; and an idea of "poetic justice" according to which it is particularly fitting when someone who attempts wrongfully to harm others somehow manages to harm himself instead. Some of this thinking might be misguided, but it surely contains a kernel of truth large and solid enough to support the principle in terms of which we are explaining the moral status of self- and other-defense: that if harm must befall some but not all members of a group, and if the existence of the situation is the fault of certain individuals in the group, then it is the guilty rather than the innocent who should suffer.

Notwithstanding J's correspondence with much commonsense thinking about the nature of justice, J might appear vulnerable to certain kinds of counterexamples. Suppose, for example, you know that Flo will wrongfully kill many innocent people in the near future if she is not prevented from doing so, that you are the only one who can stop her, and that you can prevent Flo from killing the innocent people only by killing her. You are then faced with a forced choice between Flo's life and the lives of many innocent people, and it is Flo's fault that you are so situated. In these circumstances J requires you to kill Flo now— and this despite the fact that she is not presently acting in ways that endanger the lives of others. Some people would doubtless maintain that such acts of "preemptive defense" are immoral and that J must therefore be rejected.

In considering the issue here, we must carefully separate *epistemological* questions from *moral* questions. Stated in light of our recent example, the distinction here is between these two queries: (1) Are you permitted to kill Flo, knowing that, although she is presently doing nothing to endanger others, she will kill many innocent people in the near future? and (2) Can you *know* that Flo will kill many innocent people at some future time?

Analogues of (2) could, of course, have been raised in connection with the sorts of cases we discussed earlier. Thus, we might have asked whether Victim in Thomson's example can know that Aggressor will kill her if she does not kill Aggressor first. Just as we have had good reason to ignore epistemological issues in our previous discussion, so we have good reason to ignore such questions when asked about pre-emptive defense. Moreover, once we distinguish (1) from (2) and focus on the morality of preemptive defense, there will be considerable difficulty denying that preemptive defense killings are permissible while affirming that killings are permissible in the various defense and preservation cases we have considered.

Preemptive defense cases are not the only potential sources of difficulty for J, however. Thus, suppose that Guy requires a certain kind of pacemaker to stay alive and that only one such device exists. Realizing this, Hattie, who wishes Guy dead, removes the pacemaker from Guy and deliberately swallows it. Guy has a choice: he can do nothing and die from heart failure, or he can kill Hattie, retrieve his pacemaker, and survive for many years. It is Hattie's fault that Guy is faced with this forced choice, and, hence, according to the principle put forward above, Guy is permitted to kill Hattie to save himself. Many people would doubtless resist this conclusion, however, and maintain that Guy may not kill Hattie to save his own life.

Here is a case that is even more troublesome. Again we have Guy, who requires a unique pacemaker to stay alive. We also have Izzie, Guy's doctor, who suffers from a serious vision problem. Izzie is well aware of this problem, but he resists wearing glasses out of vanity. While ministering to Guy, and without his glasses, Izzie mistakes Guy's pacemaker for a vitamin pill and swallows it. If we assume that Guy will surely die in a very short time without his pacemaker and that there is no way to retrieve it except by killing Izzie, then Guy is faced with a forced choice between his life and Izzie's. Since Guy's predicament is Izzie's fault, we must evidently conclude on the view being advocated here that Guy may kill Izzie to save himself. It is clear, however, that many would find this conclusion even more objectionable than the analogous one drawn earlier in the case of Guy and Hattie and, hence, would be even more strongly inclined to question the principle of justice we are appealing to in explaining the morality of self- and other-defense.

While the case of Guy and Izzie might be somewhat problematic, it certainly is not a clear counterexample to the position being defended here. The case of Guy and Hattie counts even less clearly against this position. That is, it is certainly arguable, at least, that Guy may kill Hattie if that is the only way to retrieve his pacemaker and save his own life. Differences in opinion regarding these two cases probably reflect very basic differences in attitude toward the matter of killing, but it seems highly doubtful that one who denies that Guy may kill Hattie to save himself is able consistently to maintain that killing to save oneself is ever morally permissible. At any rate, it is hard to see what principle might be appealed to as a means of drawing a moral distinction between the two cases recently examined on the one hand, and previously discussed self-preservation cases and self-defense cases on the other.

Summary

Since punishment as societal-defense is seen as analogous in significant respects to individual self-defense, an examination of the former's moral dimensions requires an explanation of why it is that individuals are justified in defending themselves against aggression in certain circumstances. Explaining the morality of self-defense requires that two problems be solved, both of which concern evident moral asymmetries that obtain between aggressors and their intended victims in certain self-defense situations. One asymmetry consists in the fact that, because everyone has a right to life, aggressors in standard self-defense situations act wrongly if they kill the targets of their aggression, but that, even if everyone has a right to life, intended victims in standard situations are permitted to kill the aggressors in order to protect themselves. The other asymmetry consists in the fact that, while the intended victims of aggression are permitted to exercise their right of self-defense, the aggressors are not permitted to exercise their right of self-defense if the victims fight back. A theory of self-defense must explain the existence of these asymmetries or explain them away.

One approach to explaining the asymmetries that appear to obtain in self-defense situations is proposed by Judith Jarvis Thomson. Focusing on situations in which deadly threats posed by aggressors can be nullified by—and only by—the use of deadly force on the part of their intended victims, Thomson claims that the targets of aggression in these situations have rights not to be killed by the aggressors, but that the latter have no rights not to be killed by the former. In developing her position, Thomson relies heavily on the claim that the relevant principle in the situations on which she focuses is that, other things being equal, every person has a right against every other person not to be killed by them. The argument in which she employs this principle—the central argument of her account—is unsound, however.

An alternative approach to explaining the morality of self-defense centers on the idea that targets of aggression in self-defense situations face forced choices between allowing themselves to be harmed and harming their attackers. Viewed in this way, self-defense situations are revealed as similar in morally significant respects to other-defense situations as well as to self-preservation and other-preservation situations, where neither of the latter involve defense against aggression. In all such situations, some individuals will be harmed if nothing is done, some individuals are in positions to determine who is harmed, and the existence of the situations is the fault of some of those who can be harmed. In such circumstances, justice presumptively requires that the harm be done to those whose fault it is that the circumstances exist, unless those in positions to distribute the burdens are potential recipients of the burdens, in which case they are not required but do have a right to distribute them in ways that favor themselves over the culpable parties.

This principle of distributive justice is qualified by several defeasibility conditions. One is that the harm done to those who are at fault in the relevant sorts of situations be proportional to the harm that would be done to innocent people under different distributions. A second defeasibility condition is that the harm done to the parties at fault be the minimum necessary to avoid harming innocent individuals. A third defeasibility condition is that harm not be done to innocent people who are outside the endangered group.

Chapter 3

Societal-Defense

Further Reflections on Justice

The preceding chapter's central point is that the morality of self-defense should be understood in light of principle J, which is concerned with the just distribution of burdens in certain forced-choice situations. Explaining the morality of self-defense in terms of such a principle, and thereby connecting acts of self-defense in morally relevant ways with acts that also differ significantly from acts of self-defense, is of considerable importance for the present discussion, for the goal here is to formulate a theory of punishment as societal-defense and, in doing so, to rely on analogies between societal-defense and individual self-defense. The more general and fundamental is the principle on which the proposed account of punishment as societal-defense is based, the less likely is the account to be ad hoc—to contain components specifically designed to avoid problems that would otherwise arise. A similar concern is implicit in the discussion in chapter 4, in which suggestions are made concerning the need to embed the theories of punishment examined there in more general moral frameworks.

In this chapter we will rely on J in arguing that the moral presumption against punishment is defeated when punishment serves as an instrument for justly distributing burdens under certain conditions. Before attempting to develop this position, however, we will consider whether there are principles of distributive justice that are both independent of and more firmly established than J and that apply to the situations of interest to us here. Our discussion of distributive justice will be quite limited, however. We will examine it only to the extent that is necessary for our present purposes and, as a result, many important and interesting questions about the nature of justice will be ignored. For example, we will not discuss, at least not directly, the relation between justice and liberty or equality, or whether liberal theories of justice are superior to

51

rival views. While the claims to be made about justice are important components of the theoretical framework within which the account of punishment as societal-defense is being developed, they are meant neither to be earthshaking nor to count for or against any of the theories of distributive justice that are discussed. These theories—or some of them, at least—might be quite acceptable and still be inapplicable to the situations covered by J.

Some accounts of distributive justice are exclusively forward looking, and hence the causal histories of benefits and burdens are ignored in their distribution principles. Radically egalitarian theories belong in this category, but other accounts belong there as well. As was noted earlier, theories of justice that do treat backward-looking considerations as significant typically focus on such considerations insofar as they are relevant to how *benefits* should be distributed. Thus, a view of this sort might treat the causal histories of benefits as relevant to their just distribution by implying that goods can be properly acquired and properly transferred by their owners and that, when properly acquired goods have been properly transferred, they are justly distributed. Even theories of justice that accommodate backward-looking considerations pay little if any attention to whether the causal histories of *burdens*—understood as distinct from the absence of benefits—have any bearing on how they should be distributed. According to J, of course, certain facts about the causal histories of burdens are relevant to their just distribution.

We are looking for principles of distributive justice that attribute moral significance to the causal histories of burdens as J does, and that are preferable to J as a basis for determining how those burdens should be distributed in situations of certain sorts. These days, and for some years now, references to principles of distributive justice inevitably call to mind the principles set forth by John Rawls in *A Theory of Justice.*[1] Fortunately for us, Rawls's principles have been examined in great detail and at considerable length by a host of philosophers over the years, and, hence, our discussion of them can be brief. Before saying anything about Rawls's principles of justice, however, we must consider an aspect of his position on punishment that bears directly and importantly on the view that punishment can be justified by appealing to J.

Rawls has relatively little to say about punishment in presenting his theory of justice, and the following remarks give some indication of why this is so.

> . . . the purpose of the criminal law is to uphold basic natural duties, those which forbid us to injure other persons in their life and limb, or to deprive

them of their liberty and property, and punishments are to serve this end. . . .

It is clear that the distribution of economic and social advantages is entirely different. These arrangements are not the converse, so to speak, of the criminal law, so that just as the one punishes certain offenses, the other rewards moral worth. The function of unequal distributive shares is to cover the costs of training and education, to attract individuals to places and associations where they are most needed from a social point of view, and so on. . . . To think of distributive and retributive justice as converses of one another is completely misleading and suggests a different justification for distributive shares than the one they in fact have. (314–15)

Rawls therefore regards justifying punishment as a problem of retributive justice—which he claims is completely separate from distributive justice. If he is right on both counts, then he can have a theory of justice (i.e., a theory of *distributive* justice) that is entirely forward looking, while allowing backward-looking considerations to play a role in justifying punishment. If this way of thinking about punishment is correct, then the approach being developed here—an approach that interprets the justification problem for punishment as a problem of distributive justice—is fundamentally misguided.

The distinction Rawls draws between distributive and retributive justice rests in large part on these two claims: that justice in the distribution of economic and social advantages does not depend on whether potential recipients have good characters or are morally worthy; and that justice in punishment does depend on the characters and moral worth of those punished. If we examine Rawls's rationale for the first of these claims, however, we will find that it undermines his second claim.

Rawls argues that character and moral worth should not determine how benefits are distributed because the factors that shape character and determine moral worth are "arbitrary from a moral point of view" (312). Leaving aside the difficulties associated with this line of reasoning, we can certainly apply it to justice in punishment. If the arbitrariness of the factors that determine character and moral worth imply that such considerations should play no role in determining how advantages are distributed, then—for the same reason—they should play no role in determining how punishments are imposed.

The point being made here can be put another way. Rawls denies that considerations of character and of moral worth are relevant to whether economic and social advantages are justly distributed, and he concludes that distributive justice is entirely a forward-looking matter. He does regard considerations of character and of moral worth as relevant to whether punishments are justly imposed, however, thereby allowing retributive justice to be at least partly backward looking, but he provides no very good reason for separating distributive from retributive justice in this way. In the absence of a persuasive argument in support of his claim that distributive and retributive justice are distinct concepts, his remarks also cast no doubt at all on the idea that justifying punishment is—in the final analysis—a matter of distributive justice.

Our present concern, however, is not simply to defend the general approach to justifying punishment that we are taking here. It is also to consider whether Rawls's principles of justice provide a better basis than J does for examining how burdens should be distributed in the sorts of situations to which J applies. Accordingly, let us turn to a brief examination of Rawls's principles.

Rawls states that the concept of justice with which he is concerned "applies whenever there is an allotment of something rationally regarded as advantageous or disadvantageous" (8). He places great emphasis on the distinction between, on the one hand, the justice or injustice of individual actions and, on the other hand, the justice or injustice of institutions and practices that belong to "the basic structure of society." Individual justice is composed of obligations of fairness and the "natural duty" of justice. We should note that, for Rawls, all obligations are voluntarily incurred and all are, at bottom, obligations of fairness. In contrast, the natural duties bind people without their having been incurred by actions of any sort, and there is no highly generic natural duty of which specific natural duties are manifestations. For example, people have a natural duty to help others in distress without their having done anything to incur that duty. There is also no general principle that implies both a natural duty to help others, and a natural duty of justice—where the latter "requires us to support and to comply with just institutions that exist and apply to us. It also constrains us to further just arrangements not yet established, at least when this can be done without too much cost to ourselves." (115)

The just distribution of burdens in the forced choice situations we have been discussing cannot be explained by referring to either obligations of fairness or the natural duty of justice. What justice requires of people in these situations is obviously unrelated to any natural duties of justice they might have—that is, to any duties they might have to support or further just institutions. The requirements of justice in self- and other-defense cases, in self- and other-preservation cases, and so on are not obligations at all (not in Rawls's sense, that is), and they are therefore not obligations of fairness.

When we turn to the matter of institutional justice, we encounter the principles commonly known as Rawls's "principles of justice." Rather than stating these principles in their full complexity, we will rest content with the following "General Conception" that they embody: "All social primary goods—liberty and opportunity, income and wealth, and the bases of self-respect—are to be distributed equally unless an unequal distribution of any or all of these goods is to the advantage of the least favored." (303)[2] Given that Rawls characterizes justice as concerned with allotments of advantages and disadvantages, his omission of any references to disadvantages in the General Conception, as well as in his principles, is somewhat puzzling. Assuming that his General Conception and his principles do not require supplementation in order for them to apply to distributions of disadvantages, burdens, and so on, they can be construed, and will be construed here, as implicitly incorporating factors that render them applicable to allotments of burdens.

Assuming that the forced choice situations discussed in the preceding chapter do indeed involve distributions of burdens, those situations fall within the scope of justice as Rawls characterizes it, but they do not provide occasions for applying his General Conception of justice, because the latter principle is inapplicable to individual acts of distributing benefits or burdens, and, hence, it is no substitute for J as a basis for determining the justice of individual distributions of burdens. Moreover, if Rawls's General Conception is meant to apply to institutions and practices concerned with the distribution of burdens, it appears to yield incorrect results in situations of the types to which we have applied J.

Here is why: People can surely create situations in which there are burdens to be distributed and in which these situations present societies with forced choices. Even if our various defense and preservation cases are claimed not really to exemplify these situations, the dead cow case that we considered in the previous chapter surely does. Now, unless we reject moral responsibility across the board, we must acknowledge that people can be responsible for the existence of that which societies must choose how to distribute. Assuming we want these distributions to be just and to fall within the scopes of institutions or practices that are, broadly speaking, "societal" in character, we must consider the criteria according to which these institutions and practices are to be constructed. It seems crystal clear that the criteria in question must incorporate considerations of responsibility for the existence of burdens that societies are to distribute by means of their institutions.

Yet neither Rawls's General Conception nor his principles of justice contain references to responsibility (fault, culpability, and so on). Thus, for example, if we follow Rawls's General Conception or his principles in establishing a practice within which the burdens created by the factory owner in our dead cow case are distributed, then we will focus exclusively on the maximization of equal basic liberty for all and on how future advantages are distributed if inequalities are allowed. In Rawls's view, backward-looking considerations such as culpability for past acts can have at most indirect relevance to the justice of distributions. This sort of result is surely mistaken. There can be no legitimate doubt that the factory owner's culpable negligence is directly relevant to how the burdens she creates are justly distributed.

Rawls regards his General Conception of justice and the principles to which it corresponds, as well as obligations of fairness and the natural duty of justice, as part of what he calls "substantive" justice. He contrasts principles of substantive justice to a principle of "formal" justice, which requires that

> similar cases are treated similarly, the relevant similarities and differences being those identified by the existing norms. The correct rule as defined by institutions is regularly adhered to and properly interpreted by the authorities. This impartial and consistent administration of laws and institutions, whatever their substantive principles, we will call formal justice. If we think of justice as always expressing a kind of equality, then formal justice requires that in their administration laws and institutions should apply equally (that is, in the same way) to those belonging to the classes defined by them. (58)

The principle with which Rawls associates formal justice in this passage—a principle we will call J1—requires the similar treatment of relevantly similar cases and, presumably, although Rawls's omission here is probably significant in light of his egalitarian proclivities, the dissimilar treatment of relevantly dissimilar cases. We need not worry here about whether Rawls is right in distinguishing formal from substantive justice or about whether, if there is such a distinction, J1 is in fact a part of formal justice, because, however it is interpreted, J1 seems clearly to bear importantly on matters of distributive justice, and it warrants serious consideration as a possible replacement for J.

J1 certainly seems applicable to situations of the sort to which J applies; and it appears also to yield the right results when it is applied to those situations. For example, victims and aggressors in standard other-defense situations seem to be relevantly dissimilar (which might be another way of saying that their positions are morally asymmetrical), so that a suitably situated third party would be required by J1 to treat them differently. If J1 can indeed be used as a basis for claims about justly distributing burdens in forced choice situations, then J would appear to be dispensable and should probably be abandoned. To abandon J, however, would be to reject our explanation of the morality of self-defense and, with it, the foundation of our account of the justification of punishment in terms of the idea of societal-defense.

Although J1 will in fact play a significant role in our discussion of punishment as societal-defense, it is no substitute for J. We can see this by considering the idea that J1 requires third parties in standard other-defense situations to treat the aggressors in those situations differently from their intended victims because the latter are relevantly different from the former. While all this might well be true, it says nothing about choosing in favor of the intended victims of aggression. More importantly, what we have said about applying J1 to other-defense situations gives no hint of what differences between aggressors and their intended victims are relevant and of why they are relevant.

Rawls's discussion of distributive justice, while enormously important and influential, is clearly neither the first nor the last word on this topic. We cannot engage here in anything remotely resembling a comprehensive examination of the literature of distributive justice, but, having argued that nothing in Rawls' discussion of distributive justice applies usefully to forced-choice situations to which J applies, we will very briefly consider principles discussed by some other writers concerned with the nature of justice.

According to John Hospers, justice consists in "treating each person in accordance with his or her deserts."[3] Using desert as the basis for justly distributing burdens in the cases to which J applies, however, would require specifying conditions under which individuals deserve to be burdened, and then applying these conditions to standard self-and other-defense cases, standard self- and other-preservation cases, and so on. It was in any case by way of attempting to accomplish these tasks that we developed J. Hence, the requirement that benefits and burdens be distributed according to desert cannot serve as a replacement for J. Indeed, if the former requirement applies at all to situations involving the distribution of burdens in the forced-choice situations we have been considering, then its applicability probably *presupposes* that certain determinations have been made on the basis of J.

In contrast to Hospers, S. I. Benn and R. S. Peters maintain, "To act justly . . . is to treat all men alike except where there are relevant differences between them."[4] The difficulties associated with applying this principle to the cases to which J applies parallel those involved in attempting to apply J1 to such cases. Thus, suppose we attempt to appeal to the Benn and Peters principle in standard other-defense situations. Third parties in such situations would be required to treat victims and aggressors equally unless they differ from each other in relevant ways. Even assuming that victims and aggressors are relevantly different from each other, there is nothing in the Benn and Peters principle that explains these differences and nothing that suggests that victims should be favored over aggressors.

William Frankena characterizes justice in two ways, one similar to the Benn and Peters view and the other resembling Hospers's. Thus, Frankena states that "justice is comparative,"[5] and elaborates on this theme by claiming, "Justice is treating persons equally, except as unequal treatment is required by just-making considerations (i.e., by principles of *justice*, not merely *moral* principles)."[6] But then, almost in the same breath, Frankena says, "Justice simply is the apportionment of what is to be apportioned in accordance with the amount or degree in which the recipients possess some required features—personal ability, desert, merit, rank, or wealth."[7]

For reasons given above in connection with the views of Hospers and of Benn and Peters, neither of Frankena's principles can be substituted for J. The distinction between conceptions of justice that are comparative on the one hand and conceptions that are noncomparative on the other is of course only one way in which theories of justice can be classified. Theories can also be differentiated according to the extent to which they are forward or backward looking, or egalitarian or meritarian in character, or some finer-grained classification scheme might be utilized in attempting to explain various views regarding the nature of justice.[8] However, none of the standard ways of classifying accounts of justice seem to reflect J's central idea, and standard accounts therefore cannot replace J as indicating how justly to distribute burdens in situations of the sort to which J applies.

From Individual Defense to Societal-Defense: Defensive Warfare

The preceding discussion suggests that J cannot be dispensed with in favor of various other principles of distributive justice that are endorsed in the literature. One reason certain principles are unsuitable as replacements for J is that they apply only at the level of societal institutions, whereas J is applicable at both the institutional and the individual level. If we attempt to apply J to cases of individual punishment, however, we encounter a serious difficulty to which we alluded in the preceding chapter in quoting Nathanson, because situations in which the punishment of individual offenders is being contemplated are not generally forced-choice situations. Unlike acts of self- or other-defense, say, which occur before harm is done to innocent people, punishment is after the fact. Someone faced with the decision of whether to punish a criminal would typically not be attempting to distribute harm that is unavoidable from the former's standpoint. Harm could be avoided entirely by a decision to refrain from punishing.

If, therefore, J is to play a role in solving the justification problem for punishment, it cannot be applied to the punishment of individuals. The question remains, however, whether J applies at the level of societal institutions—whether, in particular, it can be used to justify systems of punishment as instruments of societal-defense. While the concept of societal-defense is not commonly employed in the literature of punishment, it plays a central role in discussions of the morality of war. In this latter context, societal-defense is a component of national defense. A brief look at the morality of national defense will not only form a bridge between our discussions of individual self-defense and of punishment as societal-defense, but will also provide a further application of the aspect of distributive justice that underlies our discussion of the morality of defense.

Before proceeding, however, we must distinguish between national defense as a form of societal-defense, and the defensive actions that might be performed by individual combatants in warfare. Whether these latter actions are performed in self- or other-defense, they fall squarely within the scope of J. Also, while issues of proportionality, minimization, or side-effects might be especially difficult to resolve under the conditions that actually obtain in warfare, no special theoretical issues arise. In what follows, then, we will be focusing on defensive measures taken by entire nations, rather than on any individual defensive acts.

Just as defending oneself against wrongful aggression is regarded almost universally—and quite reasonably—as the clearest justification of the use of force by individuals, so defensive wars have traditionally been viewed as the ones most easily justified, if warfare is ever justified.[9] So the ideas of nations fighting wars in their own defense and of their being justified in doing so are familiar and apparently unproblematic. Yet, as we have seen, explaining why and when individual self-defense is justified is no easy matter; and the difficulties associated with producing an adequate theory of individual defense will quite obviously plague attempts at explaining the justifiability of defensive warfare. Discussions of the nature of "just wars" have suffered considerably from their lack of plausible and well-developed explanations of the morality of national self-defense.

In broad outline, at least, these explanations can be constructed rather easily by relying on analogies with individual self-defense. All we need do is view nations as sometimes faced with forced choices in the distribution of burdens whose existence is the fault of other, aggressor nations and then infer that the former have a right, other things being equal, to distribute the burdens in their own favor. Granted, one might question the idea that nations (as opposed to governmental officials, say) are capable of making choices, but we can make perfectly good sense of this idea by interpreting it in terms of analogues of the features of individuals by which they make choices. Prominent among these analogues are decision-making procedures that must be implemented by individuals who occupy a great variety of positions. For example, a nation will typically have procedures for declaring war, for the mobilization of troops when war is declared, for the production and delivery of war materials, and so on, and, while these procedures are implemented by individuals, their implementation can quite reasonably be regarded as the collective action of the nation's waging war. After all, while Franklin Roosevelt, the members of the various congresses in office from 1941 through 1945, U. S. military personnel, factory workers, and so on, all played roles in World War II, it was *the United States* that waged war.

So in virtue of there being appropriate collective analogues of individual decision making, we can make sense of nations as facing forced choices in the distribution of burdens between themselves and other nations, and we can therefore make sense of using J as a basis for justifying defensive warfare under certain conditions. The advantages of doing so become apparent when certain claims and questions about the morality of war are considered.

Thus, as Jenny Teichman points out, one form of pacifism "distinguishes between permissible and impermissible kinds of violence by drawing a line between the external and internal use of force by the state."[10] An implication of the view being advanced here, however, is that no such line can be drawn if a state's external use of force is appropriately defensive: the principle that justifies the use of force internally will also justify its use externally. Indeed, if the question of whether certain defensive wars are justified is a matter of distributive justice to be answered by appealing to J, then—regardless of whether they attempt to separate internal from external uses of force—pacifists who oppose war unconditionally are faced with either rejecting J or demonstrating that it is inapplicable to defensive warfare. Neither of these alternatives appears very promising.

In addition to providing grounds for rejecting certain forms of pacifism, J also can be used to answer other questions about the morality of warfare. For example, if what we have said about the applicability of J to self-defensive warfare is correct, then we have at hand also an explanation of when and why other-defensive warfare is justified. Such warfare is justified under conditions analogous to those under which individual acts of other-defense are, and, just as these latter acts are required under the conditions specified in J, so is other-defensive warfare required under the parallel conditions.

A final issue worth mentioning here concerns the morality of preemptive warfare. As was pointed out in chapter 2, individual preemptive acts of self-defense are justifiable on the basis of J, and we can now note that preemptive defensive warfare is justifiable as well. We acknowledged in our earlier discussion that some people might find the idea of justifiable preemptive defense objectionable, and we emphasized the importance in addressing this issue of ignoring epistemological considerations. A similar warning is appropriate here. That is, while serious difficulties are doubtless associated with coming to *know* whether some preemptive defensive war is justified, these difficulties are irrelevant to whether that war is in fact justified.

Nothing in the preceding discussion should be interpreted as implying that questions about the morality of particular wars or of particular war-related activities are easy to answer. It is, after all, one thing to determine the conditions under which wars are justified; it is quite another to determine whether those conditions are satisfied in particular cases. Questions about the satisfaction of J's proportionality, minimization, and side-effects conditions would be particularly difficult to answer in warfare contexts. To distinguish matters of principle, or theory, from matters of practice is by no means, however, to minimize the formers' importance, because even though the existence of acceptable principles by no means guarantees that their applicability and implications are clear, they are surely necessary for reasoned judgments about real situations to occur. The point of this discussion has been to show how certain considerations of distributive justice that are applicable to various sorts of cases involving individual decision making, also apply to situations in which nations are faced with decisions of whether to engage in warfare.

Punishment as Societal-Defense

We are now in a position to consider whether, by appealing to the notion of societal-defense, we can solve the justification problem for punishment. Here we will be concerned with the conditions under which societies are justified in establishing institutions and practices aimed at defending some of their members against the wrongfully aggressive acts of others.

Imagine a society S that contains a subclass S' of individuals who are both strongly inclined and quite able wrongfully to kill or injure innocent members of S and who will do so if not directly prevented from acting. Innocent members of S are therefore at risk of being injured or killed because of the inclinations and abilities of those in S'. Assume for now that S can protect its innocent members only by establishing a police force with powers of direct intervention in cases where those in S' attempt to injure or kill innocent persons, and assume also that the police are both willing and able to injure or kill members of S', if doing so is the only way to prevent innocent members of S from being comparably harmed.

If we focus on the choice facing S as a society, then we have a situation exactly analogous to the cases of individual self- and other-defense described earlier. Certain harms in the form of risks of death or injury[11] are unavoidable from the standpoint of S as a whole, but they can be distributed by S in different ways. Moreover, certain members of S (i.e., those in S') are to blame for the fact that there is unavoidable harm to be distributed. Thus, according to J, justice presumptively requires S to distribute the harm among those in S', and hence to establish a police force. Note that the choice facing S (as opposed to the choices facing members of the police force) is not whether to defend individuals against wrongful aggression. Rather, it is a choice whether to establish a police force and thereby to create significant conditional risks for the members of S' of being injured or killed by the police.

Let us now modify our example somewhat. Suppose that those in S' cannot be prevented from harming innocent persons no matter how large and diligent a police force S establishes, but that credible threats to their own well-being can deter them from doing so. Assume too that

S can pose such threats by establishing and effectively implementing a system of legal punishment and that doing so places would-be offenders at significant conditional risk of being punished. Assume finally that risks of harm to innocent people that those in S' create cannot be reduced without somehow harming the latter. Under these conditions harm is again unavoidable from the standpoint of S as a whole, though S does have some control over how this harm is distributed. A distribution involving threats of punishment will favor innocent members of S over those in S', while a distribution not involving such threats will have the opposite result. Also, since those in S' are to blame for the fact that there is unavoidable harm to be distributed, J presumptively requires S to establish a system of legal punishment.

Two points are worth emphasizing before we proceed. One is analogous to that made above in connection with S's establishment of a police force—namely, that the forced choice faced by S is not whether to punish individuals; rather, it is a choice whether to establish a system of punishment in the face of risks to innocent members of S created by those in S'. Hence, the problem noted earlier as associated with applying J to *individual* punishment (i.e., that punishment is after the fact of harm being done to innocent persons) does not arise. A second point to bear in mind is that S's choice is not simply between having a system of punishment and not having any such system. S must decide what *sort* of system of punishment justice requires, assuming it requires some such system. As was noted earlier, systems of punishment can differ from each other in various ways: with respect to whether they incorporate the death penalty, with respect to whether their punishments fit their offenses, with respect to whether they divide offenses into many distinct categories or only into a few such categories, and so on.

Some of these choices among systems of punishment are constrained by defeasibility conditions for J. For example, the proportionality condition requires that harm done to offenders within a given system of punishment be proportional to the harm that would be done to innocent people if no system of punishment were established. At the level of systems this translates into the requirement that punishments must fit crimes—a requirement that can now be seen to arise from basic and very general considerations of distributive that which are embodied in J. Punishments must be proportional to crimes in the same way and for the same reasons that any distribution of unavoidable harm satisfying the conditions mentioned in J must meet proportionality requirements. This is not to minimize the difficulties that can arise when attempting to answer questions about proportionality in particular cases, although there does seem to be a tendency to exaggerate these difficulties when the relationship between punishments and offenses is at issue; nor is it to suggest that applying proportionality considerations in the area of punishment is entirely without difficulties. Indeed, some difficulties associated with such applications will be discussed in the next section.

Along with the proportionality condition for J, its minimization and side-effect conditions must also be satisfied when the principle is applied to the choices facing S. Thus, S must select a system that results in the minimum harm to those in S′ that is necessary to protect innocent persons and must also be concerned with the harm that might be distributed to some innocent persons as side effects of protecting others. If we regard S as at least approximating a real society, then the kinds of wrongful harm that those in S′ are disposed to do might well include such widely varied activities as burglary, assault, and murder. If so, then the system of punishment selected by S must reflect these differences if the proportionality condition of J is to be satisfied. Furthermore, if it is possible to deter those in S′ from engaging in some category of wrongdoing by correlating with that class of wrongdoings a punishment less than proportionality permits, then the minimization condition of J requires that the lesser punishment be selected. In addition, if threats of punishment for given offenses will have harmful side effects for innocent persons, then this must be taken into account when assessing the moral acceptability of that system.

In this way, limits are placed on the kinds of punishments that may be correlated with different kinds of wrongdoing in a system of punishment. A system that stipulates the death penalty for burglary almost certainly violates the proportionality requirement; a system according to which premeditated murder is punishable by death might satisfy the proportionality requirement, but it might fail to meet the minimization requirement; and a system of punishment that prescribes the death penalty for certain offenses may have unacceptably harmful side effects for innocent persons. Whether a society fails to meet any of these requirements when it establishes a particular system of punishment depends on what conditions obtain in that society.

Societal-Defense and Proportionality

Because of the importance of determining the relevance of considerations of proportionality to the justifiability of punishment, our brief discussion a few paragraphs ago of proportionality and societal-defense deserves to be expanded even at the risk of some repetition.

The idea that punishments must fit crimes—call this the "correspondence thesis"—can be construed in two very different ways. On the one hand, we have the idea that the severity of particular forms of punishment must correspond appropriately to the seriousness or gravity of the specific types of wrongdoing to which they are assigned. On the other hand, we have the notion that equally severe punishments must be correlated with equally grave categories of wrongdoing, while more (less) severe punishments must be assigned to more (less) serious types of wrongdoing. These will be referred to here as the "absolute proportionality thesis" and the "relative proportionality thesis," respectively.

Thus, since murder is a more serious wrong than is theft, the relative proportionality thesis requires that murder be punished more severely than theft is. This thesis implies nothing, however, about the specific punishments that must be assigned to either category of wrongdoing. The relative proportionality thesis would presumably accommodate systems of punishment in which murderers were executed and thieves imprisoned for five years, as well as systems in which murderers received ten-year prison sentences and thieves one-year sentences. This kind of flexibility is evidently precluded by the absolute proportionality thesis, however, since it presupposes that murder, for example, is serious to a certain degree and that it must be matched by punishments that are severe to the same degree.

To ensure that the correspondence thesis does not require an apples-and-oranges comparison, and to avoid other well-known difficulties associated with certain versions of the thesis, both the seriousness of wrongdoings and the severity of punishments will be assumed here to qualify a feature that wrongdoings and punishments have in common—namely, their being harmful. The idea, then, is that a wrongdoing's seriousness reflects the harm done to those who are wronged, while a punishment's severity is a measure of the harm it does to those on whom it is imposed. Indeed, the correspondence thesis, as well as the relative proportionality and absolute proportionality theses, might simply be stated in terms of amounts or degree of harm done through wrongdoing and through punishment, thereby eliminating references to seriousness of wrongdoing and severity of punishment. Linking wrongdoing and punishment with harm in this way is problematic in certain respects, but not in respects that affect our present discussion. We will therefore assume that the severity of a punishment and the seriousness of a wrongdoing amount to the harmfulness of each.

At first glance, anyway, it would appear that if there are problems associated with incorporating considerations of proportionality into an explanation of punishment as societal-defense (or into any theory of punishment, for that matter), then these problems arise not from relative proportionality, but rather from absolute proportionality, because, after all, the relative proportionality thesis follows from J1, which appears indisputably to be a sound principle of justice, while the absolute proportionality thesis seems to lack any such foundation, and its implementation would appear therefore to require stipulating correlations between wrongdoings and punishments that are arbitrary or ad hoc. Given that the correspondence thesis cannot be interpreted solely in terms of relative proportionality and given the problems that seem to surround absolute proportionality, there is reason to wonder whether the idea that punishments must fit crimes is, in the final analysis, defensible.

Two sorts of considerations can be invoked to show that doubts on this score are less firmly grounded than they might appear to be—which amounts here to showing that the absolute proportionality thesis and, with it, the relative proportionality thesis, are indeed defensible. First we have the fact that absolute proportionality occupies an important—and reasonably unproblematic—place in the morality of self- and other-defense, and, second, there is the fact that systems of punishment have analogues in which absolute and relative proportionality work hand in hand without evident difficulty. Let us look more closely at these facts and their bearing on matters of proportionality for punishment.

First, there should be little doubt that considerations of proportionality are relevant to the permissibility of defensive acts on the part of targets of aggression in self-defense situations and suitably situated third parties in other-defense situations.[12] Furthermore, the proportionality that is applicable to these situations is absolute rather than relative. Now, our accounts of the morality of self- and of other-defense on the one hand and of punishment on the other are based on J, and the absolute proportionality thesis is simply an application of the proportionality that governs J to systems of punishment. If, therefore, we can make perfectly good sense of absolute proportionality when we apply J to self- and other-defense situations, then we are unlikely to face insurmountable barriers in attempting to apply absolute proportionality to systems of punishment.

Second, systems of punishment incorporate rules that correlate types of acts classified as offenses with types of treatments classified as punishments. Typically, at least, the offenses are ranked ordinally according to seriousness or gravity, the punishments are ranked ordinally according to severity, and, as required by J1 through the relative proportionality thesis, offenses of similar (dissimilar) seriousness are correlated with punishments of similar (dissimilar) severity. We are presently exploring the possibility of there being absolute correlations of punishments with offenses of the sort that appear to be required if acceptable relative correlations are to be established.

The features of systems of punishment we have just described have analogues for certain other systems of rules. Consider, for example, what we will call "systems of remuneration," which consist of rules correlating types of acts classified as tasks or jobs with types of treatments classified as remunerations or payments. The tasks are typically ranked ordinally according to levels of skills or responsibility required for their successful performance, while the remunerations are ranked in the obvious way. Moreover, tasks requiring similar (dissimilar) skills or responsibility are correlated with similar (dissimilar) remunerations—which is, of course, how J1 requires tasks and remunerations to be correlated. For example, members of the office staff of a university with certain skills and responsibilities might be classified as "office assistants," while those with greater skills and increased responsibilities might be classified as "secretaries," and those with still greater skills and responsibilities might be classified as "administrative assistants." One would then expect secretaries to be paid more than office assistants, but less than administrative assistants.

This expectation would be based—at least implicitly—on the idea of equal pay for equal work (and unequal pay for unequal work), which is, of course, an application of relative proportionality to systems of remuneration. If we are thinking of this appeal to relative proportionality as relevant to whether our imagined system of remuneration is just, however, then—as is the case when applying relative proportionality to systems of punishment—it appears to need supplementation by absolute proportionality. If, for example, office assistants, secretaries, and administrative assistants were being paid ten cents an hour, two dollars an hour, and three dollars an hour, respectively, then the requirements of relative proportionality might be satisfied, but the system of remuneration would certainly not be just. For the system to be just, the remunerations that are correlated with particular tasks must be fair, and the notion of fair remuneration for tasks seems to involve absolute proportionality.

This last remark should not be interpreted as implying that proper remunerations for particular tasks can simply be read off descriptions of those tasks. Clearly, various background considerations—market factors in particular—are relevant to what counts as fair remuneration for given tasks during particular periods of time. The fact remains, however, that satisfying constraints imposed by relative proportionality is insufficient by itself to make a system of remuneration just. Considerations of absolute proportionality are also relevant.

The foregoing remarks suggest that there is some cause for optimism regarding the possibility of implementing the absolute proportionality thesis for systems of punishment. Doing so, however, would doubtless require adopting a certain assumption governing the absolute proportionality thesis. We must assume that both the seriousness of wrongdoings and the severity of punishments are explicable in terms of references to harm done. As we shall see in chapter 4, however, retributivists are likely to balk at interpreting the seriousness of wrongdoing exclusively in terms of harm—or of any features of actions—because they will maintain that a wrongdoing's seriousness is at least partly dependent on the wrongdoer's culpability. This way of thinking reflects the fact that retributivists commonly interpret the fittingness of punishments to wrongdoings in terms of desert—which is not a feature of acts but is rather a feature of persons as agents. According to this way of thinking, not only are there true individual desert claims of the form "Person X deserves punishment Y for having done Z," but there are also true general desert claims of the form "People deserve punishment of type . . . for having engaged in wrongdoing of type. . . ."

We are not bound by any such retributivist constraints in correlating types of wrongdoings (or offenses) with types of punishments, however. That is, we need not interpret these general correlations in terms of desert. Hence, we can construe both the seriousness of offenses and the severity of punishments as measures of harm, and we can do so without having to regard degree of culpability as relevant to the seriousness of offenses. While it might seem that ignoring considerations of culpability in this way precludes our regarding as punishable acts in which people unsuccessfully attempt to kill or injure others, this is not in fact the case. If, as we are doing here, harm is interpreted broadly enough to include placing other people at risk of being killed or injured, then attempted murder, for example, can count as an offense in the view being proposed. In a similar vein, this view can accommodate the idea that acts of reckless or negligent endangerment are punishable without having to count considerations of culpability as relevant to the seriousness of offenses.

The suggestion being made, then, is that if the seriousness of offenses and the severity of punishments are both understood in terms of harm done and if harm is broadly construed in the manner just suggested, then the idea that punishments must be absolutely proportional to offenses is no more problematic than are appeals to absolute proportionality in cases of self- or other-defense, or in "systems" having nothing to do with punishment—systems of remuneration, for example.

It is worth emphasizing, however, that considerations of absolute and relative proportionality are insufficient by themselves to determine the moral acceptability of specific forms of punishment. Not only must the minimization and side-effect conditions be met, but moral considerations independent of J might also be relevant. For example, such considerations imply that punishing people by slowly torturing them to death would be morally impermissible even if no lesser punishment would serve equally well as an instrument of societal-defense.

Justifying Individual Punishments

Suppose that establishing a particular system of punishment P is presumptively required according to J and that the moral presumption in favor of P is not defeated by competing moral considerations. Then establishing P is *strictly* required. Does it follow that punishing individuals within P is also strictly required? If this question is interpreted as asking whether P's moral acceptability is sufficient for punishing individuals within P to be strictly required, then it should be answered negatively. That P's establishment is strictly required could imply at most that punishing individuals within P is *presumptively* required, but does the strict requirement to establish P imply even a presumptive requirement to punish individuals within P?

One might attempt to base an affirmative answer to this question on the following line of reasoning: P is justified on the grounds that it functions effectively as an instrument of societal-defense, but P's effectiveness in this regard depends on the credibility of its threats, and these threats are credible only if they are carried out in particular cases—only if individuals who ignore them are punished; hence, punishing offenders within P is presumptively required. Now suppose, however, that P is maximally credible during a certain time period. That is, suppose P's effectiveness in preventing or deterring wrongdoing during the period in question is unaffected by whether anyone is punished within P during that time. Then the preceding argument does not establish even presumptive requirements that offenders be punished within systems of punishment during times when the threats of the system are maximally credible.

A possible response to this result is that it is unproblematic. After all, it might be claimed, if punishing offenders neither prevents nor deters wrongdoing, then punishing them is unjustified, but this response is unsatisfying for reasons related to those that have made retributivism so appealing to so many people. If, for example, we knew that a vicious murderer would engage in no further serious wrongdoing regardless of whether she is punished and if we knew too that punishing her would deter no one else from serious wrongdoing, then assuming we believed that the system within which the murderer would be punished is justified, we would probably resist the conclusion that no moral presumption exists in favor of punishing her.

Is there anything within the societal-defense view that provides grounds for resisting this conclusion? The answer to this question is "yes," but to see why, we must look again at the justifications of systems of punishment.

As they have been interpreted here, systems of punishment embody threats of punishment to potential wrongdoers, but establishing a system of punishment involves more than the mere issuance of threats. In addition, threats are created: establishing a system of punishment puts people at conditional risk of being punished, and it is in this sense that establishing systems of punishment is harmful and therefore requires justification. A system of punishment is justified according to J only if innocent people would be at significant risk of injury, death, and so on, without the system and only if these risks are reduced by placing would-be offenders at significant risk of being punished. So what J requires is the establishment of mechanisms that genuinely threaten people and that will therefore be implemented in cases where the threats are ignored.

Nothing in this account implies that the risks created by a justified system of punishment are to be eliminated during times when the system's threats are maximally credible, and it is hard to see what sort of argument for eliminating them might be formulated within the context of punishment as societal-defense. Certainly, the fact that a system's threats are maximally credible during a particular period is not a sufficient reason for eliminating the system, because even during periods of maximal credibility, the threats of a system can be effective deterrents, and harm can therefore be more justly distributed within a system with maximally credible threats than within an alternative system. Notwithstanding these considerations, however, doubts might linger regarding whether justifications for punishing individuals follow from justifications of systems of punishment in the manner suggested, because, it might be claimed, a society's being justified in putting offenders at conditional risk of being punished is one thing; being justified in actually punishing offenders is quite another.

This difference is emphasized by Warren Quinn in his proposal for justifying individual punishment in terms of claims about justified threats of punishment. Central to Quinn's account is the idea that punishment is justified by virtue of its being related in a certain way (its being "functionally equivalent") to a practice Quinn calls "m-punishment" and that he claims is justified. M-punishment is imagined to work by way of devices that are programmed to "detect wrongdoing . . . , identify and apprehend those who are responsible, establish their guilt, and subject them to incarcerations (and perhaps other evils) . . . [called] mechanical punishments, or m-punishments for short."[13] An important feature of m-punishment is that, once the m-punishing devices are programmed, their instructions cannot be altered. The devices are therefore seen as serving exclusively deterrent purposes, with no suggestion that m-punishments are imposed on retributive grounds.

Along with the obvious differences between punishment and m-punishment, Quinn points out that

> real punishment involves not only creating threats but also carrying them out and therefore raises questions that do not arise in the case of m-punishment. While the dangers to potential wrongdoers may be no greater under a practice of punishment, their realization will require real persons to perform various real actions all of which will clearly stand in need of some kind of moral justification. And it may seem that no appeal to our right to protect ourselves from possible crimes could serve to establish a right to do anything about those crimes once they had become actual. But the problem is, in a way, even worse. For the right to which we appealed when activating the m-punishing devices was the right to attach *automatic* costs to crimes. But in the case of punishment we need to appeal to a right to attach costs that will have to be imposed by human agents.[14]

Quinn argues that, despite the differences between punishment and m-punishment, they "are on the same moral footing,"[15] and, in arguing for this claim, he examines the relation between being justified in forming conditional intentions—particularly intentions to punish people if they engage in wrongdoing—on the one hand, and being justified in carrying out these intentions on the other.

We need not examine Quinn's argument in any detail in order to see that his emphasis on the relation between forming and carrying out intentions is probably misguided. Some indication of his being on the wrong track is given by the fact that, if threats of punishment do indeed embody conditional intentions, then they are society's; whereas the particular acts that count as punishing offenders—the acts Quinn claims are in need of justification—are performed by individual prosecutors, judges, wardens, and so on. Hence, the relation between some X's being justified in forming a conditional intention and *that X's* being justified in carrying out that intention, does not arise in connection with societal threats of punishment.

Having distinguished between the threats (and, perhaps, the conditional intentions) of societies on the one hand and the actions of individuals who participate in punishing wrongdoers on the other, we can begin to see the importance of Quinn's point that establishing systems of punishment involves more than merely creating threats. It consists also in establishing various positions, the occupants of which are responsible for aspects of the process by which individual offenders are punished. After making this point, Quinn argues in the manner described above. He suggests that—in contrast to the mindless responses to wrongdoing that characterize m-punishment—individual punishments occur when people deliberately choose to fulfill certain conditional intentions. He claims that, despite this difference, punishment is related to m-punishment in a way that implies that the former is justifiable because the latter is.

However, an account of the justification of individual punishment much simpler than the one Quinn develops is available to him—and to us as well. This alternative account is also preferable to the original in that it omits Quinn's dubious claims about intentions. The central idea is easily stated: if establishing a system of punishment is justified, then creating certain positions that system requires, with their attendant responsibilities, is justified, and the people who occupy those positions are certainly justified in fulfilling their responsibilities—that is, presumptively justified in participating in the punishment of individuals. Moreover, assuming that systems whose establishment is justified remain justified during periods when their threats are maximally credible, those to whom the systems assign responsibilities for individual punishment remain justified in fulfilling those responsibilities.

There is a clear sense, then, in which the justification of a system of punishment with the threats it embodies is sufficient to create presumptions in favor of punishing individuals within the system. Saying this, though, is by no means to endorse Quinn's general principle that if threats are justified, then carrying out those threats is justified. Hence, the problems with Quinn's position to which this principle gives rise do not afflict the account presented here of the justification of individual punishment.

A Comparison with Other Justifications of Punishment

Punishment as societal-defense is based on a principle of justice in the distribution of burdens under certain conditions—the principle we have referred to as J. As we have noted, the use of J in justifying legal punishment satisfies at least one intuition underlying desert-based retributivism in requiring that systems of punishment satisfy proportionality conditions. It is also tempting to link J with retributivism by claiming that on both views it is somehow *fitting* that wrongdoers suffer, simply by virtue of their having engaged in wrongdoing. Indeed, we might wish to express this relationship in terms that are even more closely associated with desert-based retributivism: we might say that one whose fault it is that either he or some innocent person will be harmed receives his *just deserts* when the harm is distributed to him rather than to the innocent person. The relationship between this interpretation of desert and the retributivist's is rather tenuous and at any rate unclear, but it might provide some basis for regarding J as containing a retributivist element.

These similarities between the two positions do not go very far, however, because, as we noted in our discussion of desert-based retributivism, retributivists must surely acknowledge that one can deserve a certain treatment without anyone else's being morally required to accord the person that treatment. They are then faced with two alternatives: either take as given and absolutely fundamental the requirement that societies establish practices that inflict deserved suffering on wrongdoers, or they must provide (presumably retributivist) criteria for distinguishing individual deserts that imply moral requirements on the part of others, from individual deserts that imply no such requirements.

The first of these alternatives is, to say the least, rather unsatisfying; and, while retributivists might be able successfully to pursue the second alternative despite the associated difficulties discussed in chapter one, doing so would almost certainly require adjustments in their position. These adjustments might well lead to a principle like J, which does provide a basis for societal requirements to engage in legal punishment under certain conditions, but which generates this requirement from considerations that are ultimately independent of desert-based retributivism. In particular, it is not possible by the use of J, as it is by appealing to strictly retributivist considerations, to justify establishing a system of legal punishment when doing so has no value as an instrument of societal-defense and serves only to ensure that wrongdoers suffer.

Because the societal-defense account is a double-level theory that places considerable emphasis on forward-looking considerations at the systems level, it has a certain affinity with the deterrence view we called rule utilitarianism for punishment. An additional similarity between the two theories is evident in their accounts of the morality of individual punishment: both accounts rest on claims about individuals' being justified in fulfilling responsibilities that justified systems of punishment assigned to them. The two theories would be brought even closer together if rule utilitarianism for punishment were formulated in a way that attributed appropriate moral significance to creating threats of punishment.

These two approaches to justifying legal punishment differ in several important respects, however, because everything that rule utilitarianism for punishment implies about the moral acceptability of systems of punishment must obviously be consistent with its basic contention that societies are justified in establishing systems of punishment only if doing so is less harmful than alternative courses of action. Assuming that the harm referred to here is aggregate harm, the implications of utilitarianism can differ significantly from those of J. It might happen, for example, that if society S engages in legal punishment, its members will collectively suffer more harm than they will if no system of punishment is established. Presumably, a utilitarian must then conclude that S should not engage in legal punishment. Depending on how the harm in question is distributed, however, J might yield a very different result. In particular, if, by establishing a system of legal punishment, S distributes unavoidable harm among those whose fault it is that harm is unavoidable, then S is presumptively required to engage in legal punishment even if the members of S collectively suffer more harm than they would without legal punishment.

As we have seen, moreover, rule utilitarianism for punishment cannot accommodate certain considerations that seem clearly to be necessarily relevant to determining the moral acceptability of systems of punishment. Nothing in rule utilitarianism for punishment ensures that the rules of systems of punishment pay any attention at all to considerations of guilt and innocence, for example. Neither is there room in rule utilitarianism for punishment for the idea that systems of punishment must incorporate rules that require punishments to fit offenses. In contrast, both types of considerations are prominently present in punishment as societal-defense by way of references to fault and to proportionality.

In the preceding remarks we have compared punishment as societal-defense with retributivist and deterrence theories. We have done so in order to emphasize that, although the former is importantly different from both the latter views, it nevertheless satisfies a very plausible condition of adequacy for theories of punishment. The condition is that such theories must somehow accommodate both the forward-looking perspective of deterrence theories and the backward-looking perspective of retributivism. Before concluding this section, however, we will devote some attention to comparing punishment as societal-defense with an account that is neither a retributivist nor a deterrence theory. The account is R. A. Duff's and is presented in his important book, *Trials and Punishments*.[16] Why we are paying special attention to Duff's views at this point in the discussion should become clear presently.

Duff claims that societies have a right to punish wrongdoers under certain conditions, that wrongdoers have a right to be punished, and also that, if a society's laws are "properly justified," the society "has a strenuous duty" to enforce them (273). The meanings of these claims—as well as their interrelations—are not at all clear, however. This is partly because of Duff's tendency to use "has a right to punish" and "punishes rightly" interchangeably, even though the two expressions are commonly used in ways that are not at all equivalent (200, 207–208). In addition, the idea that criminals have a right to be punished does not seem to be interpreted as a claim right that implies the duty to punish that Duff claims societies have. Rather, the right to be punished appears to be a right to not be punished for certain purposes, and the duty to punish follows from "the duty of care and respect which the state owes to all its citizens—both the law-abiding and the criminal" (273). More specifically, societies are required to respect their members as autonomous and rational agents, and they are therefore justified in punishing their criminal members only if their doing so manifests an appropriate respect for autonomy and rationality.

But Duff also maintains, "If I use violence to defend myself against a murderous assault, I may claim that I am still treating and respecting my assailant as a rational and autonomous agent. I am responding appropriately to his voluntary and wrongful action . . ." (227). So Duff is acknowledging that harming culpable aggressors in self-defense is justified in that it respects autonomy and rationality. If the duty of care that Duff claims societies owe their law-abiding members is interpreted as implying a duty to defend them against criminals, then one might reasonably conclude that a justification of punishment on grounds of societal-defense also passes Duff's test. To be sure, Duff dismisses the idea that punishing a criminal is justifiable on grounds of self-defense because "[the punishment] follows his crime" (255). As we have seen, however, this sort of reason does not really provide grounds for denying that punishment as societal-defense is analogous to individual self-defense.

The point here is not that Duff would embrace punishment as societal-defense if confronted with the arguments advanced in this and the preceding chapter. The point is rather to suggest that the claims on which Duff's justification of punishment centers are completely consistent with—and might even provide support for—a societal-defense account of punishment.

Summary

Situations that present opportunities for distributing benefits or burdens—and in which questions of distributive justice arise—are widely varied with respect to their morally significant features. In some of these situations only the just distribution of burdens is at issue, and those in positions to distribute the burdens face forced choices regarding how to distribute them. In a still narrower range of situations it is the fault of some of the potential recipients of the burdens that there are burdens to be distributed. These are the situations to which J applies, and they include the self- and other-defense and the self- and other-preservation cases discussed in chapter two.

Are there other, more familiar, and firmly established principles of distributive justice that also apply to such cases?

An examination of principles discussed by writers on distributive justice suggests that the answer to this question is "no." Some proposed principles of distributive justice apply only at the level of institutions, practices, and so on, and hence, unlike J, are inapplicable to cases in which the just treatment of individuals is at issue. Other principles, while perhaps applicable at the individual level, are not very useful when appealed to in situations of the sorts to which J applies. For example, the principle that justice requires people to be treated according to their deserts is of little or no help to someone attempting to solve the asymmetry problems associated with cases of self- and other-defense.

In the absence of equally satisfactory alternatives, J provides a reasonable basis on which to determine how burdens are justly distributed in certain forced choice situations.

These applications of J to situations in which individuals face forced choices in the distribution of burdens have societal analogues. Among the most familiar of these are situations in which nations engage in warfare as the only way to defend themselves from attack by aggressor nations. Although determining whether specific defensive wars are in fact justified might well be a very difficult business, the general approach to making such determinations is provided by J. Too, while questions might arise about the possibility of societies' genuinely making choices regarding how to distribute burdens, such questions seem answerable by referring to societal procedures that are analogues of individual decision making.

Forced-choice situations of the sort to which J applies are also faced by societies some of whose members are willing and able to kill or injure innocent members of those societies in pursuit of their own ends. Those in the former group place the latter at risk of injury or death and are therefore at fault for creating burdens that their societies might be in positions to distribute by creating comparable risks—through threats of punishment—for those whose inclinations and abilities endanger innocent people. If societies can distribute the burdens constituted by these risks more justly by establishing systems of punishment than they can without doing so, then they are presumptively required to establish such systems.

Whether presumptive requirements to establish systems of punishment convert to strict requirements depends, largely, on whether the proportionality, minimization, and side-effect conditions associated with J are satisfied. The proportionality condition is particularly interesting because it serves as one of two bases for the idea that punishments must fit crimes. J1 supplies the other basis—a principle widely accepted as central to the concept of distributive justice. Punishment as societal-defense can therefore accommodate the idea that punishments should fit crimes by appealing to J and to J1 and without reference to claims about retributive justice.

Punishment as societal-defense lends itself to various approaches to the justification of individual punishment. Since establishing systems of punishment includes creating threats, one possible approach to justifying individual punishment would be by way of the principle that carrying out threats is justified if the threats themselves are justified. This principle is almost certainly false, however. A second possible approach relies on the claim that systems of punishment can serve as instruments of societal-defense only if their threats are credible, and the threats of a system are credible only if they are carried out in individual cases. But this claim, while probably true in general, provides no basis for punishing people within systems during times when the threats of those systems are maximally credible.

A third approach to justifying individual punishment that the societal-defense view can accommodate appeals to the idea that establishing systems of punishment includes creating positions whose occupants are responsible for various aspects of the process of individual punishment. If the systems assigning these responsibilities are justified, then fulfilling the responsibilities in particular cases is also justified (presumptively, that is).

Because punishment as societal-defense is based on J and because J embodies both forward- and backward-looking considerations, the societal-defense view is similar in certain respects both to utilitarian-based deterrence theories and to desert-based retributivism, but punishment as societal-defense also differs significantly from these other theories. In particular, punishment as societal-defense does not attempt to justify punishment in terms of claims about desert, and it does not treat considerations of deterrence as capable in and of themselves of defeating moral presumptions against punishment.

Chapter 4

Rethinking Retributivist and Deterrence Theories

Mapping the Territory

We have now examined three approaches to justifying legal punishment. In chapter 1 we took brief looks at desert-based retributivism and at deterrence theories derived from utilitarian moral theories, and in the preceding chapter, we developed a theory of punishment based on the concept of societal-defense. All of these positions have been interpreted as versions of the permissible-infringement view, in that they propose defeasibility conditions for the moral presumption against standard forms of punishment.

In this chapter we will examine some alternative versions of the permissible-infringement view. First, there are forms of retributivism that are not desert based. These are views according to which backward-looking considerations—and desert in particular—are necessarily relevant to whether punishment is justified, but that do not treat such considerations as basic. Rather, they treat them as derivable from some more basic concepts.

Second, there are deterrence theories that are not derivable from utilitarianism. According to these theories, forward-looking considerations—and considerations of deterrence in particular—are necessarily relevant to whether punishment is justified. In theories of the type to be examined, however, considerations of deterrence are not the only ones that are necessarily relevant.

Third, there is a theory that centers on the concept of deterrence but that differs from other deterrence theories in that it attempts to justify punishment in terms of claims about justified threats of punishment.

Finally, there is an account of punishment that, although not a deterrence theory, is like utilitarian-based deterrence theories in that it treats forward-looking considerations as the only ones necessarily relevant to whether punishment is justified.

Reasons will be offered for doubting that any of these views is a viable alternative to punishment as societal-defense.

Retributivist Appeals to Fairness

According to some writers, justifying retributivism by referring to desert is only an intermediate step in the direction of providing a more basic justification in terms of principles of fairness. We noted in chapter 1 that both George Sher and Jeffrie Murphy view retributivism as based on fairness; and, according to Murphy, such a position is espoused by Kant and can be constructed from aspects of Rawls's discussions of fairness. We will examine Sher's and Murphy's accounts in turn.

Sher describes his view as "a purified version of Herbert Morris' suggestion that deserved punishment annuls the unfair advantage which wrongdoers have acquired over others."[1] The crux of Morris's proposal for justifying punishment on grounds of fairness is revealed by what he says in this passage.

> . . . fairness dictates that a system in which burdens and benefits are equally distributed have a mechanism designed to prevent a maldistribution in the benefits and burdens. Thus, sanctions are attached to noncompliance with the . . . rules [which establish distributions of benefits and burdens] so as to induce compliance with the . . . rules among those who may be disinclined to obey. In this way the likelihood of an unfair distribution is diminished.
>
> . . . it is just to punish those who have violated the rules and caused the unfair distribution of benefits and burdens. A person who violates the rules has something the others have—the benefits of the system—but by renouncing what others have assumed, the burdens of self-restraint, he has acquired an unfair advantage. Matters are not even until this advantage is in some way erased. . . . punishing such individuals . . . restores the equilibrium of benefits and burdens. . . .[2]

Sher endorses Morris' position for the most part,[3] while attempting at the same time to avoid some of its difficulties. He also develops the general view in greater detail than Morris does. Thus, Sher claims that one who acts wrongly gains "a significant measure of extra liberty: what he gains is freedom from the demands of the prohibition he violates. Because others take that prohibition seriously, they lack a similar liberty.''[4] Sher argues that punishment is justified on the ground that it burdens wrongdoers in a manner that offsets the extra measure of freedom from self-restraint they gained previously.

Regardless of whether Sher's position is an improvement on Morris's, it suffers from a number of serious defects. We will consider some of these defects now, while deferring our discussion of others (specifically those pertaining to Sher's claim that his account grounds desert on fairness) until the next section.

Let us begin by noting how difficult it is to understand Sher's claim that wrongdoers acquire the advantage of an extra measure of freedom from self-restraint. This claim is peculiar for several reasons.

First, although wrongdoers might not *exercise* self-restraint in acting wrongly, this does not imply that they are free from it. They need not even be free from self-restraint regarding the particular moral prohibitions they violate in acting wrongly. Wrongdoers choose to do what some other people choose not to do, but it is unclear that, in so choosing, they free themselves from anything. We should note in this connection that, in juxtaposing claims about being free from moral restraints with claims about liberty, Sher seems to conflate ''freedom from'' and ''freedom to.'' Even if people do somehow become free from self-restraint when they engage in wrongdoing, they certainly do not acquire an extra measure of liberty: they do not thereby become free to do things that others are not free to do.

A second problem with Sher's claims about freedom from self-restraint is that they presuppose that sense can be made of fair and unfair distributions of amounts of self-restraint. Even if self-restraint could be quantified in a useful way, there seems little chance of determining whether particular distributions of self-restraint are fair. Unless such determinations can be made, it is impossible to say whether any measures of freedom from self-restraint gained by particular wrongdoers are indeed ''extra.''

A third problem with Sher's position is its dubious assumption that being free from self-restraint is advantageous. Certainly such freedom need not be instrumentally advantageous, and there is no reason at all to regard it as inherently so. Sher seems to be working with a picture of the morally upright person as one who constantly struggles with temptations to act wrongly, and who, on yielding to temptation, is not only better off in a certain respect than those who remain steadfast in their resistance to temptation, but who also gains more of a particular benefit than she ought to have. Even if this is an accurate picture of some people, its applicability to most people is surely questionable.

These difficulties with Sher's position become even more evident on asking what his account implies about punishing individuals who belong to the following categories: (1) wrongdoers who suffer severe guilt pangs after performing their immoral acts; (2) people who act wrongly on occasion, but for whom being moral is not at all burdensome; and (3) people who have divested themselves of *moral* self-restraint, but who refrain from wrongdoing out of concern for their own interests.

Even assuming that the individuals in category (1) gain an unfair advantage by their wrongdoing, this advantage appears to be offset by the burden of guilt that they acquire. Would it then be unfair to punish them on Sher's account? The people in (2), for whom acting morally is no burden, might have to struggle to act wrongly and, hence, could hardly be regarded as acquiring a benefit when they do so. Would Sher's view imply that they should be punished anyway? Finally, if being free from moral self-restraint is to have an unfair advantage over those who do restrain themselves from wrongdoing on moral grounds, then does Sher's account imply that the individuals in (3) should be punished even though they engage in no wrongdoing? If not, then the self-restraint to which Sher refers has no necessary connection with morality, and his claims about fair and unfair distributions of benefits and burdens are even more puzzling than they are when interpreted in terms of references to moral self-restraint.

The point of discussing individuals in categories (1) through (3) is not to offer counterexamples to Sher's claim that wrongdoers gain an unfair advantage over people who refrain from acting wrongly. Rather, it is to emphasize the difficulties involved in understanding that claim.

Even if the questions that have been raised concerning the types of individuals described in (1) through (3) could be answered satisfactorily, Sher's argument would not have shown that legal punishment ought to be inflicted on wrongdoers. That is, even if Sher establishes that someone ought to do something to someone to offset any unfair advantage wrongdoers might gain through their wrongdoing, nothing in his account shows that *wrongdoers* ought to have something done to them, that they ought to be *punished*, and that they ought to be punished *within a legal framework*. As Morris acknowledges after maintaining that punishing wrongdoers restores the equilibrium of benefits and burdens upset by their wrongdoing, ''the equilibrium may be restored in another way. Forgiveness . . . while not the righting of an unfair distribution by making one pay his debt is, nevertheless, a restoring of the equilibrium by forgiving the debt.''[5]

While we might question whether, on Morris's account, appealing to forgiveness is in fact a viable alternative to punishment as a means of rectifying injustices, we can recognize nevertheless that the existence of alternatives is not precluded by anything Morris says. Neither are alternatives precluded by Sher's account. Wrongdoers could certainly be burdened without punishing them—perhaps through a system of civil remedies—and some such burdens might be imposed entirely outside the framework of legal institutions.[6] Moreover, unfair distributions of benefits and burdens created by wrongdoers might be rectified by bestowing extra benefits on morally upright people and without doing anything to the wrongdoers themselves.

Much of what we have said about Sher's view applies also to Murphy's attempt to justify punishment on grounds of fairness. In his words,

> In order to enjoy the benefits that a legal system makes possible, each man must be prepared to make an important sacrifice—namely, the sacrifice of obeying the law even when he does not desire to do so. Each man calls on others to do this, and it is only just or fair that he bear a comparable burden when his turn comes. Now if the system is to remain just, it is important to guarantee that those who disobey will not thereby gain an unfair advantage over those who obey voluntarily. Criminal punishment thus attempts to maintain the proper balance between benefit and obedience by insuring that there is no profit in criminal wrongdoing.[7]

Again we have the dubious ideas that those who engage in wrongdoing benefit or avoid a burden in doing so and that their acting wrongly places them at an unfair advantage relative to those who act rightly. We also have the questionable inference from these ideas to the claim that wrongdoers should be punished by law. Despite its similarities with Sher's account, however, Murphy's contains an element that Sher's lacks—namely, an appeal to considerations of reciprocity as they appear in the context of certain views regarding the grounds of political obligation.

Murphy's position is in fact several positions rolled into one. Thus, he endorses the "basic principle" quoted above that people should not profit from wrongdoing together with the proposition that retribution prevents this from happening. He also suggests that retributivism be understood within "a quasi-contractual model . . . that seeks to analyze political obligation in terms of *reciprocity*."[8] In his more recent writings, Murphy introduces an additional element, namely, the idea that retributivism is related in a philosophically interesting way to hatred.[9]

These three claims about the nature of retributivism are not necessarily incompatible, and, indeed, Murphy connects them in various ways in his discussions, but the claims are distinct and need not be accepted or rejected as a group. For example, one might attempt to explain retributivism in terms of the principle that people should not profit from their own wrongdoing while rejecting contractual models of political obligation. In any case, we will not assume that Murphy's various claims about retributivism stand or fall together, and we will focus on his suggestion that retributivism be understood in light of a certain type of theory of political obligation.[10]

Murphy refers to Kant and Rawls as proponents of theories of the appropriate type, but it is not at all clear that Rawls's view, at least, can be adapted to suit Murphy's purposes.

Rawls's theory of political obligation centers on the idea that political obligations (obligations to obey the law in particular) are obligations of fair play, and

> The principle of fair play may be defined as follows. Suppose there is a mutually beneficial and just scheme of social cooperation, and that the advantages it yields can only be obtained if everyone, or nearly everyone, cooperates. Suppose further that cooperation requires a certain sacrifice from each person, or at least involves a certain restriction of his liberty. Suppose finally that the benefits produced by cooperation are, up to a certain point, free: that is, the scheme of cooperation is unstable in the sense that if any one person knows that all (or nearly all) of the others will continue to do their part, he will still be able to share a gain from the scheme even if he does not do his part. Under these conditions a person who has accepted the benefits of the scheme is bound by a duty of fair play to do his part and not to take advantage of the free benefit by not cooperating.[11]

Rawls also emphasizes that "The duty of fair play is not . . . intended to account for its being wrong for us to commit crimes of violence, but it is intended to account, in part, for the obligation to pay our income tax, to vote, and so on."[12]

Rawls's reason for denying that his principle of fair play applies to acts of violence is clear enough: his principle requires the fulfillment of agreements and prohibits free riding, and neither the immorality nor the punishability of murder, assault, and so on, can reasonably be explained by referring to either of these ideas. It would be odd at best to maintain that murder and other acts of violence are wrong and should be punished because they are forms of free riding, and it would be implausible to regard such acts as nothing more than wrongful failures to comply with certain sorts of agreements. Moreover, while Rawls maintains that failures to comply with the principle of fair play upset ''the equilibrium between conflicting claims, as defined by the concept of justice,''[13] he does not suggest that acts of violence also do so, and, hence, he does not suggest that such acts create an unjust distribution of benefits and burdens.

Another way to make this point utilizes Rawls's distinction between ''obligations'' and ''natural duties''—a distinction that corresponds closely to that drawn in chapter 1 between special and general obligations. Rawls interprets obligations as moral requirements that individuals incur by voluntarily acting in certain ways, and those who incur such requirements become obligated *to* other specific individuals. Requirements to keep promises and to pay debts are obligations in Rawls's sense. Natural duties, on the other hand, are moral requirements that apply to people without those people having incurred them through their actions, and that are not owed *to* specific persons. The moral requirements to refrain from homicide and assault exemplify natural duties.

For Rawls the duty of fair play is not a duty at all, but rather an obligation; or, more accurately, it is a general type of moral requirement that encompasses more specific—and familiar—obligations. Political obligations are requirements of fair play that arise when people voluntarily enter into agreements to establish mutually beneficial and just schemes of social cooperation. People fail to fulfill their political obligations by not cooperating as they agreed to—by reaping the benefits of the scheme without contributing toward the production of those benefits. People who belong to cooperative schemes, and who murder or assault their fellow members, act contrary to natural duties—not obligations. They wrong those whom they assault or murder, but not by treating them unfairly.

Furthermore, even if some acts of violence could be shown to be immoral partly by virtue of being unfair in the relevant sense, such acts would be very rare, because people who perform acts of murder, assault, and so on typically are not parties to agreements in which they commit themselves to refrain from performing such acts. In the absence of such agreements, occasions for acting unfairly do not arise. Even granting for the sake of argument that *all* acts of violence are immoral on two counts—by virtue of being harmful and also by virtue of being unfair—the question would remain whether such acts are justifiably punished because they are unfair rather than because they are harmful.

In addressing this question one must also bear in mind that paradigm examples of acts that are unfair—failures to keep promises and breaches of contract, for instance—are less likely candidates than are acts of violence for classification as punishable by law.[14]

In sum, then, the concepts of fairness and of reciprocity are central to Rawls's theory of political obligation but have nothing to do with the types of wrongdoings that seem most clearly to call for punishment on retributivist grounds—if any types of wrongdoings do. It is worth mentioning in this connection that, for Rawls, punishment is a matter of retributive justice and is entirely independent of considerations of distributive justice. It would be surprising, then, if principles that in Rawls's view determine whether benefits and burdens are justly distributed could also be used, as Murphy seems to imply they can, to justify punishment.

The point here is not to insist that, having referred to Rawls's theory of political obligation in the course of discussing retributivism, Murphy's account of retributive punishment must correspond to Rawls's theory in every detail. The point is rather that once the true roles played by fairness and reciprocity in Rawls's account are recognized, Murphy's retributivism is revealed as having little if anything in common with Rawls's political theory. Referring to the latter in an explanation of the former is therefore misleading at best.

The appropriateness of Murphy's allusions to Kant's theory of political obligation will not be examined here. But if, as Murphy suggests, Kant's view is like Rawls's in the way it relies on the concepts of cooperation and of reciprocity, then at least some of what has been said here about Murphy's references to Rawls's account will apply as well to his remarks about Kant's theory.

Even if Murphy's and Sher's fairness accounts are defective in their details, however, what about their underlying idea that the justifiability of punishment depends on how it distributes benefits and burdens? Isn't this idea the basis of the societal-defense theory of punishment?

Although the two accounts are similar in a certain respect, this similarity is superficial, and they differ from each other in ways that are fundamental. In particular, the principles of distributive justice on which each of the two accounts is based differ significantly from each other. Fairness accounts depict wrongdoers as having acquired more than their fair share of some benefit, and they regard punishment as a way of restoring a proper distribution of benefits and burdens. This way of thinking treats consideration of distributive justice as directly relevant to the justification of *individual* punishment, and it also interprets the punishability of wrongdoings as determined by their unfairness. Punishment as societal-defense does none of these things. An additional difference between punishment as societal-defense and fairness versions of retributivism pertains to the difficulty that the latter have in connecting fairness with desert—a difficulty that raises doubts regarding whether fairness accounts are genuinely retributivist in character. This last point is worth pursuing.

In one interpretation of fairness accounts desert plays no role at all. Thus, let us agree, despite the discussion of the preceding section, that wrongdoers create unfair distributions of benefits and burdens by acting wrongly and also that benefits and burdens ought to be distributed fairly. Nothing in these assumptions implies that *wrongdoers* ought to be burdened in order to effect a fair distribution—much less that they ought to be burdened *because they deserve to be*. The morally significant factors in our assumptions are, first, the idea that certain distributions of benefits and burdens are morally objectionable by virtue of being unfair; and, the proposition that such distributions should not be allowed to stand. Neither of these factors implies that people who bring about unfair distributions deserve to be burdened for having done so—or anything else about desert, for that matter.

How, then, might considerations of desert acquire the appropriate significance in fairness accounts?

Sher attempts to deal appropriately with backward-looking considerations primarily by way of the following principle of "diachronic fairness," which he labels DF3:

> For every good G, every person M, and every period of time P, if M has less (more) of G than he should during P, then M should have correspondingly more (less) of G or some related good than he otherwise should during some later period P'.[15]

Whether people have more or less of a good "than they should have" is claimed by Sher to be determined, at least partly, by whether the good has resulted from past "violations of independent standards"— from past wrongdoings.[16]

Sher's contention, however, that "retributive desert-claims clearly are grounded in something like DF3"[17] is open to serious question, because even if wrongdoers acquire more of certain goods than they should have when they act wrongly, so that they should have less of related goods at some later times, DF3 does not imply any of the following: that someone or something should see to it that wrongdoers are divested of their excess goods, that the divestment should take place through punishment—and through punishment of the wrongdoers (as opposed, say, through punishing their innocent loved ones), or that wrongdoers deserve such treatment.

There are obvious ways in which DF3 might be modified so as to yield the first two of these propositions. For example, the following clause might be added: societies are required to punish those whose excess goods are obtained through wrongdoing. To be sure, the resulting principle would likely be objectionably ad hoc. Even if acceptable when so modified, though, DF3 would remain devoid of even implicit references to desert and, hence, would not justify punishment on retributivist grounds. The short explanation of why this is so is that claims about societal requirements and individual wrongdoings—even past wrongdoings—are *act*-appraisals, whereas claims about desert are *person* appraisals, and the latter cannot be straightforwardly derived from the former. The longer explanation consists in elucidating act and person appraisals, and how they differ from each other. Some remarks on these matters are therefore in order.

If you deliberately injure someone else, and if you do so without justification, then you have done something morally wrong. By itself, however, this negative appraisal of your action implies no moral conclusions about you. For example, it does not imply that you are blameworthy for having injured the other person: after all, you may have had a legitimate excuse for doing so—perhaps an excuse arising from your nonculpable ignorance of certain moral or factual aspects of the case, nor does it follow from your action's being wrong that you have some moral character flaw or that you are a vicious person. While there are doubtless other ways in which you might be judged morally and negatively, it is hard to see how any such judgment is implied by propositions entirely concerned with the moral status of your action.

The other side of this coin is that at least some moral judgments about people need not imply corresponding judgments about the morality of their acts—as is revealed by considering cases in which people do the right things for the wrong reasons or the wrong things for the right reasons. Thus, for example, if you are in a position to save an innocent person's life easily and if you would happily watch him die but for the presence of someone whom you want to impress, then you deserve moral criticism of a sort even though, if you do save the endangered person's life, you act rightly.

Emphasizing the distinction between judgments of persons and judgments of their acts is not to suggest that the two kinds of propositions are totally unrelated. Indeed, some moral appraisals of people imply appraisals of their acts. For example, the judgment that a person is blameworthy *for performing some action* presupposes a negative moral judgment of his action: it is judging the person as an agent. There may also be less direct connections between certain kinds of person and act appraisals. Thus, even though moral judgments about the characters of individuals or about their virtues or vices include no moral appraisals of their specific acts, the former judgments must presumably be based on appropriate propositions regarding the moral status of their patterns of behavior. In any case, the fact remains that the criteria that are appropriate for morally appraising people cannot be equated with those that apply to the moral appraisal of acts, and this is reason enough for viewing the distinction between these two types of appraisals as philosophically important.[18]

Now, desert claims—at least those concerned with moral desert—belong among person appraisals rather than act appraisals. Assuming that claims about deserved punishment refer to moral desert, to say of someone that she deserves punishment is to appraise her from a moral standpoint. It seems reasonably clear too that, if people do deserve punishment, then this is by virtue of what they have done; and to say that a person deserves punishment, or any sort of treatment, for having acted in a certain way is to appraise the person as an agent. Furthermore, since judgments that people deserve punishment are morally unfavorable person appraisals, people deserve punishment by virtue of having performed acts that are somehow morally defective.

It is important to bear in mind, however, that people do not deserve any treatment simply by virtue of the moral quality of their past acts. In addition, the persons themselves must possess certain positive or negative moral features, and they must possess these features as agents. Hence, if a person deserves punishment, then this is partly by virtue of her having acted immorally and partly by virtue of her having been morally defective as an agent in performing that action.

With these remarks about the nature of desert in mind, let us return to a consideration of Sher's account.

We noted that, as it stands, DF3 implies nothing in the way of a *requirement* that wrongdoers be divested of any excess benefits they might acquire through their wrongdoing; much less does it imply that they should be divested of these benefits by being punished. Even if DF3 were modified so that it had such implications, however, it would not imply that wrongdoers should be punished because they deserve to be, because DF3—with or without the suggested modifications—

implies nothing about divesting wrongdoers of excess benefits because of their having been morally defective as agents.

Some writers—including Sher, it appears—think that as long as backward-looking considerations are relevant to whether people should be treated in certain ways, then there are grounds for regarding the treatments as deserved. In fact, however, backward-looking considerations must be of the appropriate sort to provide occasions for desert claims, and references to past wrong actions are, by themselves, not of the appropriate sort.

We can underscore this point by looking again at cases in which people owe compensation for wrongs they have done others. We noted in chapter one that those to whom compensation is owed, while having rights to compensation, typically do not deserve it. We should now recognize that, although past wrongdoings are morally significant components of such cases, their significance consists in their generating obligations of and rights to compensation. The fact that people have acted in ways that produce such obligations and rights implies nothing about deserts on their part. Even if we assume that societies are required to extract compensation from those who owe it and will not voluntarily pay what they owe, we cannot infer that such people deserve to have it extracted from them.

The foregoing discussion furnishes reasons for doubting that attempts to base retributivism on appeals to fairness can provide a framework within which the concept of desert plays a suitable role. The problems with such attempts center on the propositions that desert claims are *person* appraisals, and that appeals to fairness, at least as they occur in Sher's and Murphy's accounts, refer only to moral features of *acts*. It is worth noting in this connection that punishment as societal-defense comes closer to satisfying the relevant intuitions underlying retributivism, because punishment as societal-defense rests on principle J, which refers to individuals' being at fault in creating certain sorts of situations. Punishment as societal-defense therefore incorporates a kind of backward-looking consideration that is central to retributivism but that is not present in theories of punishment based on fairness.

Pluralistic Deterrence Theories

According to act utilitarianism for punishment, only forward-looking considerations—and considerations of deterrence in particular—are necessarily relevant to whether acts of punishment are justified. According to rule utilitarianism for punishment, only forward-looking considerations—particularly considerations of deterrence—are necessarily relevant to whether systems of punishment are justified, and forward-looking considerations are *not* necessarily relevant to whether acts of punishment are justified. Both theories turn out to be fatally flawed by virtue of their attempts to rely on forward-looking considerations alone in justifying acts of punishment and systems of punishment respectively.

The natural move for a deterrence theorist to make in response to these conclusions is to drop the exclusivity that considerations of deterrence and other forward-looking considerations possess from the two types of utilitarian deterrence theories we have considered. Those of the resulting deterrence theories that are double level would treat forward-looking considerations as *among* those necessarily relevant to whether systems of punishment are justified and might also treat such considerations as relevant—along with others—to whether acts of punishment are justified. The resulting single-level theories would imply that, while forward-looking considerations are relevant to whether acts of punishment are justified, considerations of other sorts are also necessarily relevant. Proposals for justifying punishment according to which, in addition to forward-looking considerations (including deterrent value), other sorts of consideration are also necessarily relevant to whether punishment is justified, will be referred to as "pluralistic deterrence theories."

The simplest sorts of pluralistic deterrence theories merely add prohibitions against punishing innocent people to utilitarian theories. Employing terminology some writers use to express this idea, a prohibition against punishing innocent people is added as a "side constraint" on punishment's general justifying aim of deterrence.

One difficulty with these simple versions of pluralistic deterrence theories is that they lack theoretical roots and seem therefore to be nothing more than ad hoc responses to problems that plague exclusively forward-looking accounts. If, for example, we were to supplement act utilitarianism for punishment with a prohibition against punishing innocent people, the resulting view would no longer be derivable from act utilitarianism—or from any other recognizable moral theory. Moreover, if the prohibition against punishing innocent people is interpreted as presumptive, then it cannot simply be appended to act utilitarianism for punishment, since it would carry no moral weight at all in conflicts with act utilitarian considerations. That is, if considerations of deterrence are regarded as sufficient to justify punishment—as straightforward act utilitarianism for punishment views them—then mere presumptions against punishing innocent people cannot successfully compete with utilitarian justifications for punishing them. Such presumptions would therefore turn out, in the final analysis, to be irrelevant to the justifiability of punishment. Moral presumptions can carry genuine moral weight in situations only if the considerations with which they are in conflict are themselves only presumptive.

So the prohibition against punishing innocent people contained in the simple pluralistic deterrence theories we are considering must be construed as an unqualified constraint on punishment's general justifying aim of deterrence. According to such theories, punishment is justified if it is sufficiently effective as a deterrent—except that punishing innocent people is never justified. So interpreted, simple pluralistic deterrence theories must be rejected, because it is certainly possible that punishing innocent people is justified. One can imagine circumstances in which, for example, briefly imprisoning a person who is innocent (although believed to be guilty) turns out to be the right thing to do because it happens to prevent many other innocent people from being seriously harmed. Granted, such circumstances are unlikely to occur in the real world, but their possible occurrence suffices to render simple pluralistic theories unacceptable.

The moral of this story is that, if considerations of guilt and innocence are to be combined with considerations of deterrence to form pluralistic deterrence theories, then both sorts of considerations must be interpreted as presumptive in character. We will assume, then, that for pluralistic deterrence theories to work, they must incorporate the distinction between presumptive and strict moral requirements, prohibitions, and so on. They must also imply that facts about punishment's role in deterring people from wrongdoing are capable of defeating moral presumptions against punishment. Such facts about deterrence can play this role only if employing punishment to deter people from wrongdoing is itself presumptively required.

A pluralistic deterrence theory satisfying these conditions might be rooted in a general account of the morality of acts according to which backward-looking considerations such as the making of promises and the damaging of other people's property have necessary moral significance but that also attributes moral significance to forward-looking considerations such as causing harm to others and preventing others from being harmed. Let us assume that the requirements of this theory— requirements to keep one's commitments, to refrain from causing harm to others, and so on—are presumptive. Now suppose that, if a certain person is not punished, he will do harm to innocent persons at future times, whereas he will be deterred from doing future harm if he is punished. Then, assuming that the punishment to be inflicted is itself harmful, punishing the person is presumptively prohibited. Since punishing him, however, will result in less harm to innocent persons than will result if he is not punished, punishing him can be regarded as preventing others from being harmed and as therefore presumptively required. Hence, in our imaginary theory, considerations of deterrence can defeat the presumption against punishment; and we have a single-level account of punishment that is not embedded in act utilitarianism but that nevertheless attributes necessary moral significance to deterrent value.

In evaluating pluralistic deterrence theories, we must bear firmly in mind that they are being understood here as derivable from general moral theories composed of various presumptive requirements, prohibitions, and so on. This interpretation of the theories has been adopted partly in order to provide them with theoretical underpinnings sufficiently basic and general to block the charge of their being merely ad hoc responses to problems with utilitarian deterrence theories and partly in recognition of the fact that considerations of guilt and innocence can successfully be mixed with considerations of deterrence only if both kinds of considerations are construed as presumptive. We are not questioning the central idea of deterrence theories that certain forward-looking considerations are necessarily relevant to the justifiability of punishment. We are simply insisting that this idea be provided with an appropriate theoretical home.

The thrust of these remarks is that the principles in virtue of which pluralistic deterrence theories are *deterrence* theories must be generated by moral principles that apply to situations having nothing to do with punishment. Specifically, the principle "Punishing people as a means of deterring others from wrongdoing is presumptively required" must be derivable from some more comprehensive and necessarily true moral principle in conjunction with appropriate subsidiary necessary truths. But what might this latter principle be?

If we restrict our attention for the moment to wrongdoing that consists in doing harm to others, and if we say that harm to others is prevented when people are deterred from engaging in wrongdoing, then a fairly obvious candidate for the comprehensive principle for which we are searching is "(Necessarily) preventing harm to others is presumptively required." Another possible candidate is the "lesser evil" principle that (necessarily) harming people to prevent greater harm to others is presumptively required. Whether either of these principles is capable of generating the principles that are characteristic of pluralistic deterrence theories is not altogether clear, but neither is it important here. The point is that some necessarily true moral principle must stand behind the presumptive requirement that punishment be inflicted as a deterrent to potential wrongdoers.

Parallel remarks apply to the idea that appropriate backward-looking considerations must underlie claims about the relevance of guilt and innocence to whether people are justifiably punished. What are these "appropriate" backward-looking considerations?

Earlier we imagined pluralistic deterrence theories as being embedded in accounts of morality that contain numerous and varied moral principles, some of which refer to backward-looking considerations such as the making of promises and the damaging of others' belongings. These latter considerations concern types of actions that generate the "special obligations" discussed in chapter 1. Clearly, however, the backward-looking considerations for which we are searching—those that underlie claims about the moral significance of guilt and innocence—are not of the special obligation-generating variety. We are looking for facts about the past acts of individuals that are relevant to the justifiability of harming them. Of course, we need look no further for these facts than those referred to in principle J, which concerns the just distribution of burdens in situations where the existence of the burdens is the fault of some potential recipients of those burdens.

J cannot, however, be a component of pluralistic deterrence theories if—as we have been assuming—considerations of deterrence—and the more general forward-looking considerations of which they are instances—function independently of other considerations and of backward-looking considerations in particular. In J, a certain backward-looking consideration (viz, being at fault for the creation of dangerous situations) works in combination with a certain forward-looking consideration (viz., protecting innocent people from harm). To be sure, one might accept J and use it as we have to develop an account of punishment (the one we have called "punishment as societal-defense") and then go on to insist that this latter account is a pluralistic deterrence theory. The choice of labels here is of no consequence as long as important distinctions between punishment as societal-defense and deterrence theories of the other types we have discussed are not blurred.

If someone attempting to formulate a pluralistic deterrence theory does not accommodate appropriate backward-looking considerations by way of J, then how else might she accommodate such considerations? One method is perhaps by way of the idea that the good and bad things that happen to people should have some reasonably direct connection with their responsible behavior—an idea we alluded to in chapter 2. We noted then that, according to a strong version of this principle, good things should befall those who behave well and bad things those who behave badly. Even if this latter principle is true, however, it does not embody anything remotely resembling presumptive requirements or prohibitions regarding how good and bad people should be treated. Such presumptive requirements or prohibitions are essential for pluralistic deterrence theories of the sort we are presently considering.

The general problem here is closely related to one discussed in chapter 1 in connection with desert-based retributivist theories. We noted that such theories must derive propositions about requirements to treat people in certain ways from propositions about how those people deserve to be treated, and we argued that this sort of derivation is not possible. Much the same argument is now being employed against pluralistic deterrence theories, which must also show that propositions of the form "There is a requirement (not) to accord X such-and-such a treatment" are derivable from facts about X's past behavior. If this argument succeeds, then pluralistic deterrence theories will be unable to accommodate backward-looking considerations in a manner that protects them from fatal objections to which monistic deterrence theories are vulnerable.

Deterrent Threats

We have found reasons to reject the idea that considerations of deterrence are independently relevant to whether punishment is justified. In this section we will consider another attempt to justify punishment by appealing to deterrent value—but not the deterrent value of punishment itself. The idea is rather that punishment being justified can depend on whether threats of punishment are justified, and the deterrent value of threats of punishment determines *their* justifiability. We encountered a version of this view in the preceding chapter, when we examined some of Warren Quinn's claims about threats of punishment; and his account provides a particularly good context for our present discussion.

According to Quinn, his account of punishment

> gives equal attention to two temporally distinct components of the practice of punishment. The first is establishing the real risk of punishment, creating serious *threats* of punishment designed to deter crime. The second is, of course, the actual *punishing* of those who have ignored the threats.

According to this conception, the standard theories err in assuming that the right to threaten punishment derives from the anticipation of an independently intelligible right to punish. The central idea of this conception is, in contrast, that the right to make people liable to punishment is the *ground* of our right to punish.[19]

Quinn goes on to say of his account that

it is in some ways like both standard deterrent and standard retributive theories. Like the former, it refers the justification of punishment to the goal of prevention. But unlike them, it does not try to justify *acts* of punishment as means to that end. Only the prior threats are justified in this way. (335)

These remarks plainly reveal how in Quinn's view justifying punishment is a two-stage process. The first stage consists in justifying threats of punishment by appealing to their deterrent value; and, at the second stage, punishment is justified in terms of claims about justified threats. Our focus here will be on the first stage of this process. Before proceeding with our examination of Quinn's account, some clarification of his terminology is in order.

We must first of all consider what Quinn has in mind when he refers to "the practice of punishment," because without understanding his use of this expression, we will be hard-pressed to distinguish Quinn's theory from forms of rule utilitarianism for punishment. The need for clarification here should be reasonably clear. Quinn insists that his account differs importantly from standard theories—including those derived from "rule consequentialism," which presumably includes rule utilitarianism. He regards this difference as consisting in the fact that, unlike standard rule consequentialist theories, his account justifies actual punishment in terms of claims about justified threats of punishment. But if "the practice of punishment" is interpreted by rule consequentialists as embodying threats of punishment—and nothing in the theory seems to bar this interpretation—then justifying the practice—or, better, practices or systems—of punishment includes justifying threats of punishment. Also, since, in rule consequentialist theories, acts of punishment are justified in terms of claims about justified practices, such theories can incorporate the very two-stage process that Quinn claims is unique to his account.

The primary difference between Quinn's theory and standard rule consequentialist theories appears to be that—on the former account but not on the latter accounts—practices of punishment include individual acts of punishment. That is, while standard rule consequentialist theories treat the justification of actual punishment as occurring at a level different from that at which justifying practices occurs, Quinn's theory regards both justifications as occurring at the same level. Hence, while Quinn's account involves two stages, it in not double level in the way that standard rule consequentialist theories are.

We need not worry about the significance of this difference between Quinn's theory and standard rule consequentialist theories. The preceding discussion is aimed at locating Quinn's view with respect to other, more familiar theories of punishment to which he refers in ways that call for clarification.

We must next deal with Quinn's references to a right to punish. Quinn devotes little attention to explaining what he means by a right to punish, although some indication of what he has in mind is given by his equating the question of the right to punish with ''the question how punishment can be shown not to violate a punished person's moral rights'' (336). This move, when taken together with his evidently disparaging reference to the retributivist's concern with ''a supposed duty to punish (329),'' provides some evidence that Quinn is interested in the idea of a right to punish only insofar as it implies permission to punish. If we assume that Quinn interprets the right to threaten punishment in a parallel fashion, then his position can be characterized as follows: punishment is permissible if threats of punishment are permissible; and the permissibility of threats of punishment is determined by their deterrent value (331).

But why should there be any question about the permissibility of mere threats of punishment? To answer this question, we must consider how Quinn interprets threats, and, in doing so, we can rely on the definition he provides:

> *To create (or establish) a threat against x*, in the quasi-technical sense that I intend in this discussion, is, *first, deliberately to create a real risk that x will suffer a certain evil if he does or omits a certain specified action and second, to warn x of the existence of this risk, where by these means x may possibly be deterred from the act or omission.* (335)

Earlier, we distinguished the creation of threats from the issuance of threats, and it is clear that, in Quinn's interpretation of threats, they can be created without anyone's issuing a threat. For example, you might deliberately create a conditional risk for someone (place her at risk of being harmed if she acts in a certain way), and then warn her of the risk (with the likelihood that she will thereby be deterred from acting), and yet give no indication that you are in any way connected with that risk. Under these conditions you create a threat in Quinn's sense without ever issuing a threat. On the other hand, you might threaten someone by asserting that you will harm the person if he performs a certain action, meaning to carry out the threat if he does perform that action, without creating any genuine risk to that person. You might, after all, be unable to implement the threat even though you are convinced that you can.

Issuing threats can cause harm to those threatened—by doing them psychological damage, for example—but issuing threats can also be harmless. When issuing threats is harmless, and when those who issue the threats create no genuine risk of harm to the threatened parties, the acts of threatening are not obviously immoral—not even presumptively so. At least, it is not obvious why the mere issuance of threats is presumptively wrong, if it is. If, however, a threat is issued in connection with the creation of a risk of harm for the threatened party, then the entire process can reasonably be regarded as presumptively impermissible on the ground that placing others at risk of being harmed is presumptively impermissible. Thus, suppose that you threaten to injure a person if he crosses a line you draw on the ground. Because you are both willing and able to injure the person if he does cross the line, you have placed him at conditional risk of being injured, and your having done so implies that your act is presumptively immoral.

If we follow this line of thinking, then, given how Quinn interprets threats of punishment, they are presumptively impermissible because they create risks of being harmed for those who are threatened. The question that immediately arises is whether threats of punishment—with their attendant risks for those threatened—can be permissible by virtue of their deterrent value as Quinn claims they can; or, utilizing the framework we have adopted here, the question is whether considerations of deterrence can defeat moral presumptions against creating risks of harm to others through threats of punishment.

It is of the utmost importance in addressing this question to realize that Quinn refers to two kinds of considerations as determining whether threats of punishment are justified. On the one hand, he refers to deterrence. Such references occur in the remarks quoted above, where Quinn characterizes threats of punishment as "designed to deter crime" and where he maintains that his account justifies threats of punishment in the way that standard deterrence theories attempt to justify punishment itself. If Quinn were to rest content with this sort of comparison between his view and standard deterrence theories, then his account would be open to the same objections as the latter. In particular, his account would be no more able than rule utilitarianism for punishment to accommodate the necessary relevance of considerations of guilt and innocence to the permissibility of placing people at risk of punishment.

Quinn claims, however, that "the right to create the threat of punishment is . . . grounded in a right of self-protection" (336). Deterrence is a forward-looking concept, and self-protection is at least partly forward-looking, and the two concepts might bear other significant similarities to each other, but the existence and nature of these similarities should not be taken for granted. Indeed, if the account of self-protection developed in chapter 2 is correct, Quinn's suggestion that his proposal for justifying threats of punishment on grounds of self-protection is similar to deterrence theories is at best misleading. As we shall see, the underlying problem here is that Quinn devotes almost no attention to the important and difficult problems to which claims about rights of self-protection give rise.

The particular right of self-protection of greatest interest to Quinn is the

> right to protect ourselves by placing would-be criminals under real threats. This right is akin to, but in some ways different from, the right of self-defense and the right to construct protective barriers. (341)

One difference between Quinn's right of self-protective threats of punishment on the one hand and the right of self-defense on the other, is that the former is a right to create risks of injury, death, and so on to others, while the latter is a right to injure or kill others. If, however, people do indeed have a right to injure or kill wrongful aggressors under certain conditions, then they presumably have a right to defend themselves against risks of being injured or killed that others wrongfully create by placing the latter at risk of being injured or killed.

For example, suppose that some person threatens you with injury if you perform a certain action and that she is both willing and able to carry out her threat. Suppose too that, if you did act and she injured you for doing so, she would act immorally. Finally, suppose you threaten her with injury if she injures you for acting, that you are willing and able to carry out your threat, and that your threat nullifies hers and is the only way to nullify it. Then the person who threatens you wrongfully places you at risk, and you protect yourself from that risk by creating a comparable risk for her. Surely, if people have a right to injure others in self-defense, then you have a right to create a risk of injury to the person who threatens you in the circumstances we are imagining. If threats of punishment—along with the risks they create—are self-protective in the way Quinn claims they are, then there is reason to believe in the existence of a right of self-protective threats of punishment.

As we have seen, however, explaining the morality of self-defense is a very difficult matter, and most if not all of this difficulty is inherited by the idea of a right of self-protective threats. To see why this is so, let us again consider self-defense situations of the sort described in chapter 2. These are situations in which it is clear that people are permitted to injure or kill others as the only way to prevent the latter from injuring or killing them. If, as part of our explanation of the moral dimensions of such situations, we say that the defenders have rights not to be injured or killed by the aggressors, then the question arises whether the aggressors in these situations have a right not to be injured or killed by the defenders; or, if we say that the defenders have rights to protect themselves from being injured or killed by the aggressors, then we must wonder whether the aggressors have rights to protect themselves from being injured or killed by the defensive actions of the defenders.

It should be reasonably clear that parallel issues of comparable difficulty arise in connection with the idea that people are permitted to create risks for others as a means of defending themselves against the risks that the others have created. If we say, for example, that people have rights not to be placed at risk of being killed, then people who threaten others defensively—and who are willing and able to carry out their threats—would seem to violate the rights of those whom they threaten. If we wish to distinguish defensive threats from aggressive threats, then we need a theoretical framework within which to do so. Hence, Quinn might be correct in claiming that there is a right of self-protective threats of punishment and that this right is akin to the right of self-defense, as well as to certain other rights of self-protection, but while his being correct might locate the problems associated with justifying threats of punishment in the proper context, the problems themselves would remain unsolved.[20]

In order to develop and defend a theory of punishment based on the idea of a right of self-protective threats of punishment, a theory of self-protection is required. Such a theory would likely provide—or at least suggest—accounts of the similarities and dissimilarities among the various rights of self-protection to which Quinn alludes (assuming there are such rights), and it would doubtless reveal that, contra Quinn, threatening punishment is no more open to justification on grounds of deterrence alone than is punishment itself.

The "Republican Theory"

The "republican theory" of punishment is a component of the comprehensive theory of criminal justice developed by John Braithwaite and Philip Pettit in their book, *Not Just Deserts*.[21] Their account of punishment is consequentialist in that it treats forward-looking considerations as the only ones necessarily relevant to whether punishment is justified. It is not a utilitarian-based deterrence theory, however, because the particular forward-looking considerations on which it centers are different from those associated with utilitarianism. More specifically, while utilitarian theories require the maximization of pleasure, happiness, preference satisfaction, and so on, the republican theory requires maximizing the extent to which "dominion" is respected. In this view, then, the presumption against punishment is construed as arising from punishment's role in invading the dominion of those punished; and as defeasible by punishment's role in protecting the dominion of potential victims of would-be wrongdoers.

Braithwaite and Pettit explain the concept of dominion in terms of the concept of negative liberty, with the latter defined as follows: "An agent enjoys negative liberty . . . if and only if he is exempt from the constraints imposed by the intentional or at least the blameworthy actions of others in choosing certain options" (61). The concept of dominion is then defined in this way:

A person enjoys full dominion . . . if and only if
1. she enjoys no less a prospect of liberty than is available to other citizens.
2. it is common knowledge among citizens that this condition obtains, so that she and nearly everyone else knows that she enjoys the prospect mentioned, she and nearly everyone else knows that the others generally know this too, and so on.
3. she enjoys no less a prospect of liberty than the best that is compatible with the same prospect for all citizens (64–65).

These definitions are less clear than they might appear at first glance, however. In the first place one must wonder why enjoying dominion requires enjoying only the prospect of liberty rather than liberty itself. Second, there is the question of what work condition 2 is meant to do—particularly if enjoying dominion is no different from possessing dominion. In this latter connection, could "belief" and "believes" be substituted for "knowledge" and "knows"—and, if they could not, then why not?

Perhaps most worrisome, however, is the way that Braithwaite and Pettit use the notion of a constraint differently on different occasions. Sometimes constraints are interpreted as requirements of a sort, as in the statement that ". . . constraints may be entirely abstract. . . . An example would be the requirement that . . ." (29). At other times, however, constraints are construed as a type of obstacle or hindrance, as in the statement ". . . the liberty [i.e., the absence of constraints] to f means . . . that you are not prevented from f-ing" (61). In the first interpretation, negative liberty is equivalent to freedom as permissibility, while in the second it amounts to freedom as ability. Given that people are clearly able to do all sorts of things that are impermissible and are permitted to do things that they cannot do, these two types of freedom are significantly different from each other. The result is a serious ambiguity in the definition of "liberty," which in turn produces an ambiguity in the definition of "dominion." This latter ambiguity has implications for the sorts of things that require justification by virtue of being invasions of dominion.

Thus, for example, Braithwaite and Pettit regard punishment as requiring justification in virtue of "the cost of dominion involved in punishing the offender, in jeopardizing the security of those who are dependent on him for their upkeep or welfare, and in putting before people at large the prospect of suffering such punishment" (78). Jeopardizing someone's security or presenting her with the prospect of being punished, however, will hinder the person's choices in only certain cases, and dominion will be invaded in only those cases if liberty is equated with freedom as ability. If, however, liberty is interpreted as permissibility and if threats of punishment are contained in laws that prohibit acts of certain types, then presenting a person with the prospect of punishment necessarily limits the person's liberty and invades his dominion.

Additional difficulties arising from the republican theory's claims about dominion are revealed by examining a certain type of hypothetical case. Suppose that consideration is being given to establishing laws that prohibit acts of a certain type, and that threaten to inflict suffering on the families of individuals who perform acts of the prohibited type. Suppose further that the suffering to which families of wrongdoers are subject is restricted in these respects: it is imposed only on the young children of wrongdoers, and it consists in the infliction of pain that is momentary and that has no effect whatever on the children's future lives. Suppose finally that threats to inflict such suffering are enormously effective as deterrents.

As was noted above, merely placing someone in jeopardy of being treated in undesirable ways need not invade that person's dominion, and, hence, the threat of inflicting pain on the children of offenders would not necessarily invade the dominion of either the offenders or of their children. Given Braithwaite and Pettit's definitions, however, it is not even clear that actually inflicting pain in the situations we are now imagining would necessarily invade anyone's dominion, and if inflicting such pain does not invade dominion in a particular case, then the republican theory provides no moral grounds for avoiding such inflictions—particularly given that these inflictions deter others from invading dominion. Perhaps results like these are avoidable, but whether they are is impossible to determine from the definitions provided by Braithwaite and Pettit.

Although this lack of clarity regarding the nature of dominion creates problems for the republican theory, its most serious difficulties have a different source.

Recall our earlier discussions of act utilitarianism for punishment and of rule utilitarianism for punishment. We noted that both theories are incapable of accommodating the necessary relevance to whether punishment is justified of certain backward-looking considerations—considerations of guilt and innocence in particular. Given that our discussion of this objection focused entirely on the consequentialist character of utilitarian-based theories and was independent of their being utilitarian consequentialist accounts, one might suspect that all consequentialist theories—including the republican theory—would be vulnerable to this same objection.

Braithwaite and Pettit appear to recognize that they must deal with this point, and they argue that their view does adequately accommodate considerations of guilt and innocence. In their words,

> Assume, as seems only reasonable, that if the criminal justice authorities are guided by the target of promoting dominion, then it is occasionally going to seem desirable, even if the possibility is not announced, that some innocent party should be framed and penalized for a crime; it will at least seem desirable whenever such an individual trespass promises to maximize the overall promotion of dominion. Assume further that there is a chance that such state invasion of dominion—perhaps also its justification—will be suspected by many people and that if it occurs with any frequency, there is a near certainty of this. . . .
>
> We argue that under those minimal assumptions it does not make sense for the agents of the system of criminal justice to pursue the goal of promoting dominion in an exclusively direct fashion. . . . The reason is that

once it becomes a matter of common suspicion that the authorities use the promotion of dominion to justify particular invasions, then the dominion of ordinary people in the society is jeopardized . . . (76).

This argument is clearly reminiscent of two parallel arguments that we considered in connection with act utilitarianism for punishment and rule utilitarianism for punishment. We imagined proponents of these theories as respectively claiming that, in the real world, acts of punishing innocent people or rules allowing them to be punished would not be justifiable on utilitarian grounds. We also pointed out that, even if true, such claims are irrelevant to the objection that they are supposed to meet, because the objection is theoretical and not practical in nature. It concerns the inability of utilitarian-based theories to accommodate the *necessary* relevance of certain backward-looking considerations; and this objection is not met by pointing out that such considerations can be relevant in certain circumstances by virtue of the conditions that happen to obtain in those circumstances.

This same reply is applicable to the argument advanced by Braithwaite and Pettit in the remarks just quoted. That is, even if their theory would not countenance framing and punishing innocent people under the stated assumptions, the fact remains that their theory treats considerations of guilt and innocence as morally significant only contingently, by way of connections they have with invasions of dominion in actual situations. Hence, their argument does not address the problem raised here, which concerns the evident inability of the republican theory to account for the moral significance necessarily possessed by considerations of guilt and innocence.

Other things said by Braithwaite and Pettit, however, do seem to address the problem in question. Specifically, they point out that utilitarian theories of punishment can exclude punishing the innocent "only if the agents of the [criminal justice] system believe that people's happiness is jeopardized by the unease created when they recognize that someone known to be innocent will be occasionally punished" (76). They then claim that

Our criticism of utilitarianism in this regard was that since the importance of such unease in the happiness stakes is a contingent empirical matter, there is little or no guarantee that agents will hold the required belief. Notice now that this criticism cannot be brought against our own position. It is true as a matter of how dominion is defined—it is part of the very concept of having dominion—that a person cannot enjoy dominion fully if she perceives or suspects that the agents of the state . . . will not be scrupulous in respecting her rights (76).

These remarks are problematic in several respects, however. First of all, as was pointed out above, the definition of "dominion" to which Braithwaite and Pettit allude is objectionably unclear—certainly too unclear to serve the purpose intended for it in the preceding passage.

Second, even assuming that the concept of dominion were clearly explicated by Braithwaite and Pettit, the remarks quoted above would be insufficient to show that punishing innocent people cannot be justified within the republican theory. As they themselves point out in considering other kinds of cases in which the republican theory might seem to justify immoral legal practices, the issue turns on whether engaging in such practices "promises to maximize overall dominion" (76). This same remark applies to the question of whether the republican theory of punishment allows innocent people to be punished: it does so if such punishment maximizes dominion.

Third, even if openly framing and punishing innocent people would necessarily invade dominion, not all the ways in which innocent people can be made to suffer within systems of punishment necessarily involve such invasions, and for those that do not, the fact that innocent suffering occurs is at most contingently relevant to whether punishment within the systems in question is justified. Suppose, for example, that the framing of innocent people is done secretly, so that no one "perceives or suspects" that it is done; or recall our example in which pain is occasionally inflicted on the young children of wrongdoers with the result that people who would otherwise invade dominion are deterred from doing so. Given how Braithwaite and Pettit define "dominion," it is far from clear that anyone's dominion is necessarily invaded by the practice in question, and it is therefore unclear whether this practice has any moral significance at all within the republican theory of punishment. So Braithwaite and Pettit's claims about necessity—even if understandable and true—do not meet the objection raised here about the need for any proposed account of punishment to treat considerations of guilt and innocence as necessarily relevant to whether punishment is justified.

As we noted above, this last result is not surprising, because for the republican theory is consequentialist in character: whether punishment is justified is determined by whether it results in a maximization of overall dominion. Like rule utilitarianism for punishment, it is a theory according to which the only considerations necessarily relevant to whether systems of punishment—or laws formulated within such systems—are justified are forward looking, and considerations of guilt and innocence are backward looking.

Summary

Some retributivists, although incorporating references to desert in their theories, don't treat desert as basic. Rather, they attempt to provide a more basic justification for punishment in terms of claims about fairness. The idea is that wrongdoers acquire more than their fair share of benefits of a certain sort, thereby creating an unjust distribution of benefits and burdens; and a proper distribution is restored when wrongdoers are punished. The details of this type of position differ among its various versions, but most, if not all, are defective in certain central respects. Specifically, they fail to establish requirements that unfair distributions of benefits caused by wrongdoers—assuming that there are such distributions—be corrected by burdening the wrongdoers, that wrongdoers be burdened by being punished, that wrongdoers *deserve* such treatment, or that wrongdoers be punished within institutional frameworks.

Part of the reason for this compound failure of fairness accounts is that, while commonly classified by their proponents as forms of retributivism, they furnish no explanation of how considerations of fairness are related to the concept of desert. Indeed, given that fairness views focus exclusively on moral requirements, duties, and other features of actions, they evidently imply nothing about deserts, which are features of persons as agents rather than of actions.

Just as there are versions of retributivism that are not desert based, so there are deterrence theories that are not equivalent either to act utilitarianism for punishment or to rule utilitarianism for punishment. Some of these deterrence theories are pluralistic in the sense that they treat forward-looking considerations as only among those necessarily relevant to whether acts or systems of punishment are justified, with appropriate backward-looking considerations—considerations of guilt and innocence in particular—also regarded as morally significant. A centrally important task facing anyone proposing such a theory is that of providing a principled basis for attributing moral significance to considerations of guilt and innocence; and it is at least unclear that this task can possibly be accomplished.

An alternative to both utilitarian and pluralistic deterrence theories is provided by the idea that actual punishment is justifiable if threats of punishment are justifiable, and the justifiability of threats is determined by their deterrent value. However, appeals to considerations of deterrence alone offer no more hope of justifying threats of punishment than they offer when the justification of acts or systems of punishment is at issue. Interpreting threats as self-protective rather than as mere deterrents might well avoid the difficulties associated with purely deterrent threats, but the adequacy of such an interpretation as the basis of a theory of punishment is impossible to determine without an account of the morality of self-protection.

According to the republican theory, punishment is justified to the extent that it maximizes dominion. Like utilitarian-based deterrence theories, the republican theory is consequentialist in character, and it is therefore seriously defective in some of the same respects that other consequentialist accounts are. Specifically, it treats considerations of guilt and innocence as morally significant only in the presence of certain facts about dominion, and, hence, it cannot accommodate the idea that such considerations are necessarily relevant to whether punishment is justified.

Chapter 5

Punishment as a Societal Right

The Nature of Moral Rights

In this chapter we will examine the idea that justifying legal punishment consists of demonstrating that societies have a *right* to punish wrongdoers. This approach to solving the justification problem for punishment can be formulated within either the no-infringement or the permissible-infringement view, and we will consider both of these alternatives here. In order even to comprehend (much less to evaluate) the idea of a societal right to punish, however, we must understand what moral rights are.

Let us begin our consideration of the nature of moral rights by noting that the rights of interest to us in this section are claim rights rather than liberty rights, and general rights rather than special rights. As was pointed out in chapter 1, the claim rights of individuals imply corresponding requirements—obligations in particular—on the part of others. In contrast, liberty rights are simply liberties or permissions: they are equivalent to the lack of obligations on the part of their possessors, and imply no obligations in others. We also noted earlier that special rights are conferred on individuals by the voluntary acts of others who thereby obligate themselves to the former, as when people who borrow money confer rights to be repaid on their creditors and obligate themselves to repay what they have borrowed. No such acts of conferral are required for the possession of general rights, however, and rather than being held against some specific individuals but not others, they are held against "the world at large." The rights to life and to privacy are general in this sense, and it is with rights of this type that we are concerned in this section.

According to some philosophers, rights and obligations are two sides of a single coin: not only do all rights imply obligations, but all obligations imply rights.[1] There are reasons for doubting that rights and obligations are "correlative" in this very strong sense, however, and one reason is that at least some rights arguably imply liberties on the part of their possessors as well as obligations on the part of others. These rights are evidently exemplified by the various rights to "freedom of"—to freedom of association, freedom of religious practice, and so on. These are all rights to do things and will be referred to here as "active." In contrast to active rights are one's "passive rights" that others act or that they refrain from acting. If, for example, there is a right not to be killed or a right to be aided when in distress, then these are passive in character.

If active rights do indeed imply liberties, then not all rights are equivalent to their implied obligations, although those that are not may be equivalent to combinations of appropriate obligations and liberties. Thus, for example, the following schemata might be regarded as explaining active and passive rights respectively: X has a right to do Y if and only if X is permitted or at liberty to do Y and others are obligated not to interfere with X's doing Y; X has a right that others act (refrain from acting) in certain ways if and only if others have obligations to perform (refrain from performing) those actions.

Having acknowledged the possibility that at least some rights are composed of diverse normative elements, the natural next step is to consider the idea—associated with Wesley Newcomb Hohfeld's analysis of legal rights—that moral rights can be composed not only of liberties and obligations, but also of "powers" and "immunities." Wide variations in theories of rights result from differing views regarding the composition of rights. They range from the relatively simple and recently mentioned accounts that equate rights with obligations, to complicated theories according to which all rights are composed of various intricate arrangements of obligations, liberties, powers, and immunities.

How are we to choose among these general kinds of theories? This question can doubtless be approached in various ways, but we will proceed as follows: we will assume that rights make a significant and *distinctive* contribution to moral theory—that moral theories that can accommodate rights are essentially different from those that cannot; we will assume too that an account of rights must clearly reflect this contribution in its internal structure; we will propose an explanation of the distinctive theoretical role played by rights; and we will sketch an account of moral rights in light of this explanation. Let us begin by examining some assumptions regarding the nature of rights and of obligations under which rights do not contribute distinctively to moral theory.

Consider again the schemata mentioned above as possible ways in which to explain active and passive rights respectively. According to the schema for passive rights, these rights are nothing over and above certain obligations. If the liberties referred to in the schema for active rights are interpreted as they normally are, then active rights are explicable entirely in terms of references to obligations. That is, if we follow conventional practice among philosophers, then we will equate "X is permitted to do Y" with "X is not obligated to refrain from doing Y and, perhaps, X is not obligated to do Y." The proposed explanation of active rights will then look like this: X has a right to do Y if and only if X is not obligated to refrain from doing Y and, perhaps, is not obligated to do Y, and others are obligated not to interfere with X's doing Y.

Now consider some account of moral obligation—act utilitarianism, for example. We then have the proposition that actions are obligatory just in case the aggregate value of their consequences is greater than that of the consequences of alternative actions. Suppose that, in a given situation, the consequences of some action you are contemplating and the consequences of its nonperformance are of equal value. Then, presumably, you are obligated neither to perform the action nor to refrain from performing it. Suppose too that the consequences of others not interfering with your performance of the act are better than the consequences of their interfering. Then, given the explanation of active rights under consideration, we can infer that you have a right to act.

Note, however, these two related features of your action: first, it is morally insignificant according to the lights of act utilitarianism, and, second, the obligations of others not to interfere with your action are unrelated, except perhaps accidentally, to features of your action—something that is surely to be expected, given that your action is utterly lacking in moral significance. The general result is that, according to the views presently under consideration, people have rights to act whenever their actions are morally insignificant and others are obligated to refrain from interfering with those actions. Indeed, this sufficient condition for the possession of active rights is necessary too if the liberties referred to in our proposed schema for active rights are equated with the lack of obligations to act as well as to refrain.

The preceding discussion is aimed at illustrating how rights fail to play a distinctive role in moral theory if they are interpreted in a certain way. The following remarks by Joel Feinberg suggest an approach to establishing that rights do play such a role.

> When a person has a legal claim-right to X, it must be the case (i) that he is at liberty in respect to X, i.e., that he has no duty to refrain from or

relinquish X, and also (ii) that his liberty is the ground of other people's *duties* to grant him X or not to interfere with him in respect to X.[2]

Feinberg's statement resembles our schema for active rights, but it differs from the latter in a respect that is relevant to our present discussion. For part (ii) of Feinberg's account makes the interesting—and puzzling—claim that one person's liberties can be the *ground* of duties in others. This claim is both interesting and puzzling because Feinberg interprets liberties in the usual way—as the absence of duties—and it is extremely difficult to understand how the simple fact of one person's being without duties can be the ground of duties in others. The problem is that liberties can fill the role ascribed to them by Feinberg only if they have a kind of moral significance entirely missing from standard permissions. In other words, for condition (ii) of Feinberg's definition to be satisfied, some liberties must be morally significant and, hence, not equivalent to the absence of duties.

Suppose now that rights—or active rights, at least—incorporate liberties that are morally significant in the sense suggested by Feinberg's explanation. That is, these liberties are such that, when possessed by given individuals, they are the ground of obligations in others. Then these liberties might well provide the raw materials for constructing an account of how rights play a distinctive role in moral theory. In any case, we will develop such an account here. This account can fairly be called ''traditional'' because of how it unites much contemporary thinking about rights with that of early natural rights theorists. According to this traditional view, only moral theories that adequately accommodate rights are capable of attaching appropriate moral significance to freedom (liberty, autonomy, self-governance, and so on)—to the sovereignty or dominion that people have within certain areas of activity.

We noted above that general rights are rights that individuals possess without the actions of others having conferred them on those individuals. We also pointed out that the rights of interest here are general *claim* rights—which is to say that they are associated with obligations of certain sorts. By itself, however, this feature of rights implies nothing about right holders being sovereign within certain areas of activity. Thus, for example, your general property rights correspond to obligations in others not to damage your belongings, not to interfere with you in your use of them, and so on, but the existence of these obligations might be explained in light of a theory of rights that has nothing whatever to say about individuals having sovereignty with respect to their property. One might, for example, follow those who equate rights with obligations whose fulfillment is "directly beneficial";[3] and one might apply this view to various general rights, including rights to property, without the slightest suggestion that general right holders are sovereign within areas of activity.

Establishing the proper connection between general rights and individual sovereignty goes hand in hand with determining how correctly to characterize the obligations implied by general rights. For someone who accepts the traditional view of rights, an obvious candidate for these obligations is suggested by H. L. A. Hart, who maintains, "General rights have as correlatives obligations not to interfere."[4]

If what Hart says is true, then it would appear that all general rights are active—they are rights to do things. However, a consideration of the nature of certain rights whose existence seems entirely uncontroversial—such as rights to property and to privacy—reveals that they very definitely imply obligations other than those of noninterference that Hart seems to have in mind. For instance, by virtue of your property rights, others are obligated not to do things with your belongings regardless of whether their actions interfere with any of yours. For example, if without your permission someone uses your house as a short cut to hers, knowing that you leave your front and back doors unlocked, then that person violates a property right of yours, and she does so even if you never learn of her trespassing, you suffer no losses as a result, and, in general, your present and future behavior is unaffected. In an analogous fashion, your privacy rights require others not to spy on you by peeking beneath the drawn shade of your bedroom window regardless of whether their secret spying interferes with your activities in any way. Since in both of these cases rights violations can occur without any interference taking place, it follows that obligations of noninterference are not the only ones implied by rights.[5]

We can arrive at a more adequate characterization of the obligations implied by rights by returning our attention to the concept of individual sovereignty. Assuming that there are property rights, for example, and that people are therefore sovereign with respect to the disposition of their own belongings, it is certainly reasonable to say that property owners are at liberty to dispose of their property as they see fit and that others are obligated to refrain from interfering with them as they do so. We should also recognize, however, that sovereignty with respect to property implies more than liberties on the part of property owners and obligations of noninterference on the part of others. At bottom it consists of the idea that decisions regarding the disposition of a person's belongings are properly that person's to make—that she is at liberty to make them, and others are obligated not to arrogate such decisions to themselves.

Individuals can act contrary to such obligations of nonarrogation in a variety of ways, some of which involve no interference with the activities of those whose sovereignty they invade. For example, when people secretly use your house as a short cut, they fail to respect your sovereignty even though their actions interfere with none of yours, because in walking through your house they arrogate to themselves decisions that are yours to make regarding the disposition of a portion of your property. This point can be put another way: having sovereignty with respect to property implies being at liberty to do certain things with one's belongings—to use them, destroy them, and so on; when these things are done to a given person's property by other individuals— when they "take liberties" with her belongings—then they invade an area within which she is sovereign.

If we now think of property rights as corresponding to the sovereignty that individuals have regarding their own belongings, we can infer that these rights imply liberties on the part of property owners, as well as two types of obligations on the part of others. These are obligations not to interfere with the specific actions that property owners are at liberty to perform and obligations not to arrogate the performance of such actions to oneself. If we now extend this idea to all general rights, so that they all correspond to areas within which individual right holders are sovereign, it follows that rights imply appropriately specified liberties, as well as associated obligations of the two types just described.[6]

Consider the right to privacy, for example, which corresponds to the sovereignty that individuals have regarding the disposition of certain kinds of information about themselves. What should happen to such information is a matter to be decided by those whom the information is about, and others are obligated not to arrogate such decisions to themselves. Just this kind of arrogation occurs in our secret spying example, because for even though those who spy on you interfere with none of your activities, they do arrogate to themselves decisions that are yours to make regarding whether certain information about you is acquired by them. Analogous remarks apply to other rights. Thus, one would violate an important right of yours if she secretly sterilized you, for example, even if you were restored to a fertile condition immediately thereafter, so that her action had no affect on your actual or potential behavior. As in our property right example, the sterilizer in this last case would violate rights of yours by arrogating to herself decisions in an area of activity within which you are sovereign.

Let us suppose, then, that general rights can be explained entirely in terms of liberties on the part of right holders and two kinds of obligations on the part of others. As we noted earlier, liberties are normally interpreted as ordinary permissions and, hence, as equivalent to the absence of obligations, but we also pointed to the possibility of there being liberties that, as Feinberg suggests, are the grounds of obligations and that are therefore morally significant in a way in which ordinary permissions cannot be. Indeed, it appears that the concept of liberties that, when possessed by given individuals, are the grounds of certain obligations in others is just what we need to flesh out our characterization of individual sovereignty.

The idea, then, is that sometimes people are obligated to act or forbear *by virtue of* the liberties possessed by others, and that this sort of relation between liberties and obligations cannot obtain if the concept of liberty involved is seen as explicable entirely in terms of the concept of an obligation. It is no part of this suggestion, however, that obligations are in any way reducible to liberties—whether morally significant or not. We will treat the concept of a morally significant liberty as explanatorily on a par with the concept of a moral obligation, with the two related in the following way: necessarily, an individual is at liberty, in the morally significant sense, to perform some action only if (but not if) the individual is obligated neither to perform nor to refrain from performing that action.[7] Having rights therefore implies having moral discretion to act or forbear within certain areas; and having a right to act is incompatible with being required to act. Not surprisingly, this last point bears importantly on the question of whether punishment is justified on the ground that societies have a right to punish wrongdoers.

What Would a Societal Right to Punish be Like?

Our discussion of rights has focused on the general claim rights of individuals. When we turn our attention to the idea of a societal right to punish, however, we seem to be concerned not with individual rights, but rather with rights of collections of individuals. We must therefore pay some attention to the question of whether there are such things as collective rights. We must also consider whether, if there is a collective right to punish, it is a claim right or a liberty right and whether it should be understood as general or as special. We will address all three of these issues, beginning with the first.

The question of whether societies and other collections of individuals can possess moral rights is reminiscent of the more familiar question of whether collections of individuals can possess moral responsibility.[8] In both cases the applicability of a moral concept to collections of individuals seems to presuppose that collections possess certain features that they are incapable of possessing. Thus, moral responsibility evidently requires intentionality and the attendant concepts of belief and desire, and it is hard to see how collections of individuals—understood as distinct from the individuals comprising collections—can have intentions. Similarly, if we say that rights to do things, such as punishing wrongdoers, presuppose the capacity to *exercise* those rights, then we seem to be connecting the possession of such rights with abilities to reach decisions and make choices. It is at least unclear whether collections per se are capable of deciding and choosing.[9]

We should note, however, that if collections are incapable of possessing rights because they cannot engage in decision making, then—arguably—they are also incapable of being obligated, or otherwise morally required, to act for similar reasons. Indeed, if, as seems plausible, X's being obligated *to* Y implies a right of Y against X, then if there are no collective rights, then no one can be obligated *to* collections. It would then follow that people cannot be obligated to their countries, to the companies that employ them, and so on. The point here is not that collections clearly can be obligated to act or that individuals clearly can be obligated to collections. The point is rather that a great deal must be given up if we reject the idea that collections can have rights on the ground that they are incapable of the sort of decision making required for them to be able to exercise—and, hence, possess—rights to act in certain ways.

Moreover, it is far from obvious that collections per se must be capable of decision making in order for them to possess rights. As we suggested in the previous chapter when considering whether it is literally true that nations—as opposed to their individual members—can make choices, appropriate analogues of the features of individuals by which they make decisions might well suffice. As was noted in our earlier discussion, prime candidates for these analogues are decision-making procedures that can be implemented by individuals who fill certain roles in the collections. For example, societies that contain systems of punishment will almost certainly have procedures according to which guilt or innocence is to be determined, and yet these determinations are actually made by individual judges and jurors. To be sure, on closely examining this idea of analogues of individual decision making, we might well conclude that collections per se can only possess the analogues of individual rights. We might further conclude that a complete defense of the idea that societies have a right to punish wrongdoers would require an account of moral rights that accommodates moral *collective* rights, but there is no reason to regard such considerations as capable by themselves of undermining the whole idea of a collective right—including the idea of a societal right to punish.

Let us assume, then, that there are such things as collective rights that are similar to individual rights in significant respects, but that also might differ from individual rights in other respects. Let us also acknowledge that this supposition almost certainly implies another, namely, that there are appropriate collective analogues of individual action and decision making. We then turn to the question of whether, if there is a collective right to punish, it should be understood as a claim right or as a liberty right.

If the latter, then the existence of a societal right to punish implies only that societies are permitted to punish wrongdoers in the sense that they are not obligated to refrain from doing so. Societies are also permitted to punish wrongdoers if they have a claim right to do so, but the existence of a societal claim right to punish would also imply obligations of noninterference. Although writers concerned with the idea of a societal right to punish do not always specify whether this right is being interpreted as a claim right or as a liberty right, most appear to have the former interpretation in mind. We will therefore assume here that, if there is a societal right to punish, then it is a claim right rather than merely a liberty right. Let us now consider whether this claim right should be interpreted as a general right or as a special right.

As we have seen, individual special rights are rights that are conferred on individuals when others act in ways by which they obligate themselves to the former. In contrast, individual general rights can be possessed by individuals without having to be conferred on them by any self-obligating acts performed by others. Analogously, special *collective* rights would presuppose the existence of appropriate self-obligating acts on the part of something or someone, while general collective rights would not presuppose any such acts.

Let us assume for the moment that there is a societal right to punish. If this right is special, then it is conferred on societies by the performance of self-obligating acts—presumably on the part of members of those societies, and the most obvious candidates—perhaps the only candidates that are even remotely plausible—are the various sorts of acts that philosophers have claimed are the grounds of more general political obligations. If, for example, the members of a society consent, tacitly or expressly, to be governed by some political authority, then, arguably, they consent to the establishment and implementation of mechanisms required for the maintenance of social order—mechanisms such as police forces and systems of punishment.

We clearly cannot engage here in a discussion of the various ways in which accounts of the grounds of political obligation might provide reasons for believing in a special societal right to punish. Our purposes are served by pointing out that some such account must almost certainly be developed and defended by anyone claiming that there is a special societal right to punish, and also that successfully defending such an account would involve enormous difficulties.[10] In the face of these difficulties we will assume that, if there is a societal right to punish, then it is general rather than special.

What we have said so far about the idea of a societal right to punish applies to this idea regardless of whether it is construed as a version of the no-infringement view or as a version of the permissible-infringement view. In further examining the idea of a right to punish, however, we must divide our discussion in a way that reflects basic differences between the no-infringement view and the permissible-infringement view. We will examine the former in the next section and the latter in a subsequent section.

The Right to Punish as a No-Infringement View

Earlier, passing reference was made to criticisms that philosophers have leveled against various forms of the no-infringement view. Despite these criticisms, however, versions of the view retain their supporters, prominent among them being A. John Simmons, who argues in favor of a forfeiture version of the no-infringement view. Examining Simmons's position is particularly appropriate here, since it is unquestionably the most fully developed and successful contemporary attempt to establish the existence of a societal right to punish as a version of the no-infringement view.

Simmons argues along Lockean lines—and on the basis of claims about rights being forfeited by wrongdoers—that, under certain conditions, civil societies not only have a liberty right to punish offenders, but this right is exclusive, in the sense of not being possessed by members of those societies, and is therefore "the effective equivalent" of a *claim* right to punish wrongdoers.[11] Simmons's argument is both carefully crafted and philosophically rich, but certain of its central components seem open to serious question.

In broad outline Simmons's argument proceeds as follows.

(S1) People have a variety of natural rights, and when these rights are infringed by others, the latter forfeit certain of their own rights.

(S2) When people forfeit rights, others acquire liberty rights to accord them certain, previously impermissible, treatments as punishments.

(S3) In civil societies, individual rights to punish offenders are alienated, and portions of individual claim rights of "self-government" are transferred to governments. As a result, civil societies acquire (effective equivalents of) exclusive claim rights to punish.

(S4) The existence of a societal right to punish is therefore established.

We can develop a refined version of this argument by raising some questions about S1 through S3 and considering how Simmons answers them.

The references to forfeiture in S1 and S2 locate Simmons's position squarely within the no-infringement view; and they also invite some familiar questions regarding the notion that rights are forfeited by those who infringe the rights of others. It is certainly natural to ask, for example, which of their own rights people forfeit when they infringe the rights of others—whether in particular the rights forfeited are the same as or different from those infringed; whether rights once forfeited are lost forever; whether rights can be partially forfeited or forfeited in degrees; and whether some rights are inalienable and, hence, impossible to forfeit. Simmons is doubtless aware that accounts such as his invite such questions, but, while he suggests at least partial answers to some of them, his answers are not always clear or satisfying, and, given the importance of the idea of forfeiture to his account, he devotes surprisingly little attention to answering the objections that have been raised against it in discussions of rights.

Simmons's position regarding which rights or sets of rights are forfeited when rights are infringed is a particularly good case in point. It is impossible to determine from his account whether, for example, armed robbers forfeit all or part of their property rights, all or part of their right to liberty, all or part of their right of self-government, or all or none of the above. The problem here is thrown into sharp relief when considered in light of our sovereignty account of rights. Thus, shall we say that people who purportedly forfeit rights by acting in certain ways thereby lose all sovereignty within the areas of activity that correspond to those rights? For example, would people who forfeit their rights to privacy or to property lose their liberties to make any decisions regarding the disposition of personal information about themselves or about their belongings? If the answer to these questions is "yes," then a theory of punishment based on forfeiture will have great difficulty giving substance to the idea that punishments should fit crimes. If, on the other hand, sovereignty can be partly forfeited, some explanation is required regarding which parts of sovereignty are forfeited by the performance of particular acts. Yet it is very difficult to see how this might be done in a manner that is not blatantly ad hoc.

The sovereignty account of rights might be mistaken, of course. Regardless of how rights should be interpreted, however, the fact remains that the plausibility—indeed, the intelligibility—of claims about rights being forfeited depends heavily on what rights are, and an account of the right to punish based on the idea of forfeiture is at best incomplete if not embedded in a theory of rights.

Not only does Simmons claim that wrongdoing results in the forfeiture of rights, but he also maintains, as is stated in S2, that any right forfeited is a right not to be accorded some treatment *as punishment*. The reasoning behind this last claim is clear enough. Assuming that, say, murderers forfeit their right to life, then it might seem that others have liberty rights to kill them for any reason whatever. At the same time, however, an account of forfeiture would evidently be defective if it implied that one who forfeits her right to life thereby becomes fair game for anyone else who happens to be bent on homicide.

Simmons clearly realizes that the restriction he places on forfeiture (i.e., that it is of rights not to be accorded certain treatments as punishments) might be considered ad hoc by some people; and, in anticipation of this charge, he offers the following defense.

> . . . we often *voluntarily* transfer rights to others only to act for certain reasons (e.g., you may give your doctor the right to act during your upcoming surgery as he thinks best—but only when he acts for medical reasons, as opposed, say, to his acting for financial reasons or to enhance his professional reputation). If we may voluntarily create a situation where others have rights to act only for certain reasons, it seems plausible to suppose that nonvoluntary forfeiture might result . . . in rights to harm another only for certain reasons. . . . the unfairness to others that would be involved in allowing the criminal to *retain* his full complement of rights is unfairness only to those who *obey* the relevant rules.[12]

But even if these remarks lend some support to the idea that people can forfeit rights not to be accorded treatments for certain reasons—and this is not at all clear—they by no means establish that reasons relating to punishment are the ones applicable to forfeiture through wrongdoing. Perhaps wrongdoers forfeit rights not to be treated in certain ways as retribution, as a deterrent to others, or as a means of justly distributing benefits and burdens—none of which necessarily implies anything about punishment. In any case, we can now see that S2 must be understood in a way that reflects Simmons's claim that individual rights to punish are rights to act for certain reasons, within certain contexts, and so on.

We must also recognize that, for Simmons, people who acquire liberty rights to punish are more than merely permitted to punish offenders, because he maintains that "each person has a full claim right to freedom from (noncompetitive) interference, provided he acts within the constraints of the moral law";[13] and the conjunction of this claim right of self-government with the liberty right to punish "rules out most kinds of interference, and constitutes a reasonably substantial right."[14] Simmons also denies that interpreting the right to punish as a liberty right implies that punishment is morally indifferent, because

> ... in the case of the wrongdoer ... the punishment is not only permissible but *deserved*. ... Where it is true both that someone deserves a certain treatment and that it is permissible for us to treat him in that way, we have good moral reason to act.[15]

Needless to say, these claims raise at least as many questions as they answer—for example, questions about the existence of a right of self-government, about the role of desert in Simmons's account, and about the nature of the "good moral reasons" to which the remarks just quoted refer.

As Simmons characterizes it, the claim right of self-government appears to be a right to run one's own life as one pleases, free from noncompetitive interference by others, provided that one's self-governing acts are morally permissible. That there is such a right is certainly doubtful, however, as can be seen by considering various ways in which people can interfere noncompetitively with the permissible acts of others without needing any justification for doing so.

Thus, suppose you want to photograph my house from a particular spot and that there is room for only one person at that spot. Then if someone arrives at that spot ahead of you, you have no grounds for complaint, since the interference with your acts is competitive. You would have grounds for complaint, of course, if the other person beats you to the picture-taking spot by knocking you unconscious, because then the interference would be noncompetitive and morally wrong. Suppose, however, that I interfere with your act of photographing my house by building a high fence that completely hides the house from your view. I would then be interfering noncompetitively with a morally permissible act of yours—which seems to count as an infringement of your right of self-government—but I surely need no justification for building my fence simply because I thereby interfere with your picture-taking endeavors, from which it follows that my interference infringes no claim right of yours.

One might maintain, of course, that my building the fence is competitive interference with your actions and, hence, does not infringe your right of self-government, but then the questions arise as to what to count as noncompetitive interference and whether the obvious candidates for this sort of interference can plausibly be thought of as infringements of a right of self-government as opposed to more specific rights not to be treated in certain ways. If, for example, I prevent you from photographing my house by breaking your camera, then my interference infringes claim rights of yours and is presumably noncompetitive, but breaking your camera infringes your property rights. If I prevent you from taking pictures by killing you, then my interference again infringes a claim right of yours and is again noncompetitive, but killing you infringes your right to life. Whether, in addition to infringing your property rights or your right to life when I break your camera or kill you, I also infringe some more general claim right of self-government, is at the very least unclear.

The point being made here can be put another way. Claim rights to property, privacy, life, bodily integrity, freedom of association, and so on can all be thought of as rights of self-government in certain areas. For example, the right to property can plausibly be viewed as a right of self-government relative to one's belongings—a right to use them as one pleases, at least within certain limits. Similarly, the right to privacy can be construed as a right of self-government relative to personal information about oneself—a right to determine who has that information—again, within certain limits. Of course, parallel interpretations of the rights to life, body, integrity, freedom of association, and so on are also possible, but the existence of such rights of self-government in certain areas does not imply that there is some generic right of self-government that encompasses the areas to which the more specific rights of self-government apply. An *argument* is needed in support of the existence of a generic right of self-government—particularly when the existence of such a right plays a role as important as the one assigned to it by Simmons—and Simmons supplies no such argument.

When we turn to Simmons's claims about there being good moral reasons to punish wrongdoers, it is important to bear in mind that—as Simmons himself acknowledges—having a good moral reason for action need not imply having a duty to act. Indeed, it is not at all obvious that someone's having good moral reasons to act implies that it is in any way incumbent on that person to act,[16] and even if having good moral reasons to act does sometimes imply being obligated to act, arguments are required in support of the idea that deserts give rise to such reasons—or to any sort of good moral reasons to act.[17] These questions about good moral reasons and about deserts also arise in connection with S3, of course—as do analogues of other issues raised above in relation to the idea that individuals have a right to punish offenders.

By virtue of its reliance on the notion of forfeiture, Simmons's position is a version of the no-infringement view, and, because his position is so carefully crafted and defended, its being seriously problematic partly by virtue of its reliance on claims about forfeiture casts considerable doubt on the possibility of justifying punishment within the framework of the no-infringement view. In any case, lacking more plausible versions of the no-infringement view than Simmons provides, we will now turn to an examination of the permissible-infringement view. After developing a particular variant of this view, we will consider whether the idea of a societal right to punish fares any better if formulated within the framework of the permissible-infringement view than it does when interpreted as a form of the no-infringement view.

The Right to Punish and Permissible Infringements

A central component of the permissible-infringement view is the idea that, if rights are permissibly infringed, then the rights are only presumptive. In this view, although punishing people involves treating them in ways that infringe their presumptive rights, such treatments can be morally permissible, all things considered, on particular occasions. On such occasions the presumptions carried by moral rights are defeated by conflicting moral presumptions that, in the circumstances, are more stringent. The many and varied proposals for justifying punishment offered by philosophers past and present—retributivist and deterrence theories in particular—can therefore be regarded as attempts to produce acceptable defeasibility conditions for the moral presumption against punishment. As we saw in chapter 1, however, moral presumptions can be defeated either permissibly or prescriptively, and this distinction is extremely important when considering permissible infringement forms of the idea of a societal right to punish. An expansion of our brief, earlier discussion of these two types of moral defeaters is therefore called for.

There is a familiar account of defeasibility conditions for presumptive moral considerations—of moral defeaters—that, because of its association with the writings of W. D. Ross, we will call the Rossian view.[18] For reasons that will emerge presently, this view is more easily stated for presumptive requirements (prohibitions and so on) than for rights, and we will therefore focus initially on moral considerations of the former type.

One component of the Rossian view is that moral defeaters of given presumptive requirements are themselves presumptive requirements that compete with the former in a kind of struggle for normative supremacy. According to this way of thinking, presumptive requirements are defeated when—and only when—they are balanced or overridden by competitors: presumptive requirements balance each other when they are equally stringent or "weighty," and one presumption overrides another when the former is more stringent or weighty than the latter. In the Rossian view, moreover, if one presumptive requirement overrides another, not only is the defeated presumptive requirement prevented from becoming a requirement *simpliciter*, a *strict* requirement, but its defeater does convert to a strict requirement.

Here is how this interpretation of moral defeaters might apply to a particular sort of case: If you promise to do A and also to do B, then you are presumptively required to do A and presumptively required to do B. If A and B are incompatible, then each of these presumptive requirements functions as a competing defeater with respect to the other. If other things are equal in this particular situation, then the two defeaters balance each other, and neither presumptive requirement converts to a strict requirement. Suppose, however, that your doing A would cause considerable harm to befall innocent people while your refraining from doing A would harm no one—and other things are equal. Then the harmful nature of A is a moral defeater that prevents the presumptive requirement to do A from becoming strict by overriding it, and it thereby creates a strict requirement to refrain from doing A.

According to the Rossian view of defeasibility conditions for presumptive requirements, a presumptive requirement to perform some particular act can be defeated only by another presumptive requirement.

However, there is reason to regard this conception of moral defeaters as overly restrictive. Thus, suppose that some culpable aggressor will harm you unless you defend yourself by inflicting a similar harm on the aggressor. Arguably, people are presumptively required to refrain from harming others, but, other things being equal, the presumption against your harming the aggressor is defeated in this case. Yet your defending yourself is permissible, rather than morally required. The defeating consideration in this case is therefore permissive rather than prescriptive, and, hence, it cannot be accommodated by the Rossian account.

The notion of a permissive defeater is also useful in the area of supererogation. Thus, according to the received view, supererogatory acts are morally significant but neither required nor prohibited; and clear instances of such acts are those in which people risk serious harm to themselves in order to prevent comparable harm from befalling others. Assuming that people are presumptively required to prevent others from being harmed, then the notion of a permissive defeater is needed to explain why helping people in dire straits is sometimes supererogatory rather than either strictly required or prohibited.[19]

The distinction between prescriptive and permissive defeaters is useful not only in explaining the moral dimensions of self-defense and of supererogation, but for more mundane cases as well. This can be illustrated by returning to an example employed in chapter 2. Suppose that you have promised an acquaintance to teach her how to drive. Suppose, too, that in the course of the lessons your acquaintance becomes verbally abusive. She insults you, your family, your friends, and your pets, and, even though you are a skillful and conscientious driving instructor, she directs nasty criticisms at your teaching ability. Now, it seems clear that you are presumptively obligated to continue with the lessons you promised to provide, but it seems equally clear that your discontinuing them is permissible, all things considered. In this case, then, your acquaintance's bad behavior functions as a permissive defeater of your presumptive obligation to deliver on your promise.[20]

The distinction between prescriptive and permissive defeaters is analogous to the distinction some writers draw between "rebutting" and "undercutting" defeaters.[21] A rebutting defeater of presumptive reasons for believing some proposition p provides a presumptive reason for rejecting p, whereas an undercutting defeater of presumptive reasons for believing that p removes the presumption in p's favor without supplying any reason for rejecting p. Analogously, a prescriptive defeater of a moral presumption in favor of performing some action provides a moral presumption against performing that action; whereas a permissive defeater of a moral presumption in favor of acting eliminates that presumption without creating a presumption against the act being performed.

Let us suppose that, along with prescriptive moral defeaters, there are also permissive defeaters, which generate permissions rather than strict requirements. Then the task of providing defeasibility conditions for the presumption against infringing rights through punishment includes determining whether any such conditions that do exist are conditions for prescriptive or permissive defeaters. If, for example, we were to conclude that considerations of desert can defeat the presumption against punishing people, we would then face the question of whether punishing deserving individuals should be thought of as required or as merely permitted.

With the foregoing discussion of permissible infringements and of moral presumptions and their defeaters in hand, we can return to the idea of a societal right to punish. Having argued that the no-infringement view is not very promising as a framework within which to explain this idea, let us now consider whether the permissible-infringement view might furnish a more supportive environment for the idea of a societal right to punish. As we will see, although a potentially troublesome question regarding right-to-punish theories arises regardless of whether they are formulated within the permissible-infringement or the no-infringement view, it arises in a particularly striking way within the former view. This question is whether a society's having a right to punish wrongdoers is incompatible with its being required to do so. In examining this question, we will interpret the permissible-infringement view as embodying the presumptive/strict distinction for moral rights as characterized in this and the preceding section.

We have argued that, given certain plausible assumptions regarding the interrelations among rights, obligations, and permissions, the permissible-infringement view appears to be inconsistent; but that inconsistencies are avoided if the distinction between presumptive and strict rights, obligations, and permissions is adopted and employed in a certain way. In this latter connection, we will assume that the rights referred to in general principles should be interpreted as merely presumptive, and that presumptive rights entail only presumptive permissions on the part of right holders, and presumptive obligations on the part of others.

So, in asking whether societies have a right to punish wrongdoers, we are asking about the existence of a *presumptive* right to punish, and in addressing this question we must bear these two points clearly in mind: first, that presumptive considerations are not only defeasible, but they can also function as defeaters of other presumptive moral considerations; and, second, that—at least if rights are interpreted according to the sovereignty account—when one right takes precedence over another presumptive consideration in a conflict situation, the former functions as a permissive rather than a prescriptive defeater with respect to the latter.

Thus, if your presumptive right to act conflicts with another's presumptive right not to be treated in a certain way and if your right defeats the other person's, then, other things being equal, you have a strict right to act—from which it follows that your acting is strictly permissible but from which it does not follow that your acting is strictly obligatory. In contrast, if your presumptive obligation to act conflicts with a presumptive obligation to refrain from acting and if your obligation to act defeats your obligation to refrain, the result, other things being equal, is a strict obligation to act. Indeed, if your presumptive obligation to refrain is permissibly defeated by your presumptive right to act and if no other morally relevant considerations bear on the case, then you are not strictly obligated to act. You could be strictly obligated to act only if your presumptive obligation to refrain were prescriptively defeated (for example, by a presumptive obligation to act) and, by hypothesis, you are not so obligated.

The upshot of the preceding remarks is that, if societies have a presumptive claim right to punish offenders, then in cases where this right defeats the presumptive rights of criminals not to be punished, and when no other moral considerations are relevant to the case, societies are not strictly obligated to punish them. But why, one might then ask, cannot some presumptive rights—presumptive claim rights, that is—*prescriptively* defeat other presumptive considerations? A partial answer to this question is that presumptive rights differ from presumptive obligations at least partly by virtue of their differing roles as defeaters of conflicting presumptive considerations. If a putative presumptive right were capable of functioning as a prescriptive defeater, then it would in fact be a presumptive obligation rather than a presumptive right.[22] This reply only partially answers the question at issue because it presupposes an explanation of the nature of claim rights and of how they differ from obligations, which is like our sovereignty account. We need not insist that such an account is correct in order to recognize that the implications of there being a claim right to punish cannot be determined without an understanding of what rights are—an understanding that goes well beyond recognizing the relations of claim rights to liberty rights and of liberty rights to obligations.

We should note too that punishment theorists who make a special point of affirming the existence of a societal right to punish presumably have a concept in mind that differs significantly from that of an obligation to punish. Certainly, Simmons's account yields an interpretation of the right to punish that, as far as the possessors of this right are concerned, is entirely permissive in character. Whether Simmons and others who believe in a societal right to punish would wish to formulate their accounts so that this right incorporates an obligation to punish is unclear, however. This unclarity results in part from the tendency of right-to-punish advocates to say little about the nature of rights beyond distinguishing claim rights from liberty rights.

Another source of unclarity in this area is the unfortunate tendency of right-to-punish advocates to use ''(exercises) a right to punish'' as if it were interchangeable with ''punishes rightly.'' Simmons does this, and so, as we noted at the end of chapter 3, does R. A. Duff.[23] This sort of usage is very likely to obscure the difference between rights and obligations, since there is a clear use of ''acts rightly'' that ties it logically to ''complies with an obligation,'' and, under this interpretation, ''acts rightly'' is not equivalent to ''(exercises) a right.'' The concept of a right is far too complex to be dealt with so sketchily in discussions in which it plays the central role that theorists who employ the idea of a societal right to punish assign to it.[24]

In any case, we can go no further here in considering the idea of a societal right to punish. We will close by noting that, if the sovereignty account of rights is correct, then having a right to punish is incompatible with being required to punish; and if the proposal for justifying punishment developed in chapter 3 is also correct, then legal punishment is presumptively required, and there is no such thing a societal right to punish.

Summary

The idea of a societal right to punish can be located within either the no-infringement view or the permissible-infringement view. In order to produce viable variants of the idea within either of these views, however, a detailed and defensible account of moral rights is required, and a useful concept in terms of which to explain what rights are is that of individual sovereignty within certain areas of activity. Sovereignty within these areas consists of liberties that, unlike ordinary permissions, are morally significant in the sense of grounding obligations in others.

Questions about the acceptability of this sovereignty account aside, without some well-developed and supported explanation of the nature of rights, claims about rights central to proposals for justifying punishment are seriously problematic.

Problems with the idea of a societal right to punish interpreted as a no-infringement view are revealed by examining a particularly appealing version of that view, namely A. John Simmons's right-to-punish theory.

Problems with the idea of a societal right to punish interpreted as a permissible-infringement view center on certain assumptions regarding the interrelations among rights, obligations, and permissions—assumptions that seem to imply that the idea of a right being permissibly infringed is inconsistent. Demonstrating that rights can be permissibly infringed therefore requires that grounds be provided for either rejecting these assumptions or qualifying them appropriately. One approach to this task relies on the distinction between presumptive rights, obligations, and permissions on the one hand and strict rights, obligations, and permissions on the other and on the claim that there is no inconsistency in the idea of permissibly infringing presumptive rights. When applied to punishment, this way of thinking furnishes a basis for claiming that punishing wrongdoers is permissible when doing so infringes only their presumptive rights.

With standard forms of punishment understood as infringing presumptive rights, the justification problem for punishment is that of providing considerations capable of defeating moral presumptions against punishment. Since such defeating considerations (''defeaters'') can be either prescriptive or permissive, a proposal for solving the justification problem must specify which of the two types of defeaters it incorporates.

If, therefore, a theory based on the idea of a societal right to punish is formulated as a version of the permissible-infringement view, then it must specify whether a society's right to punish wrongdoers prescriptively or permissibly defeats presumptions against infringing rights through punishment. If the latter, then—given the nature of permissive defeaters—a society's right to punish wrongdoers is incompatible with its being required to punish them. Hence, there is no such thing as a societal right to punish if, as is argued in this book, rights are permissive rather than prescriptive defeaters, and societies are required to punish wrongdoers as a matter of societal-defense.

Chapter 6

Societal-Defense and Capital Punishment

Justifying Capital Punishment in Principle and in Practice

As one would expect, the problem of justifying capital punishment has many features in common with the problem of justifying punishment in general. Thus, capital punishment infringes the rights of those punished, or so we are assuming here, and the question arises whether such infringements are morally permissible. As is the case with other forms of punishment, this latter question divides into two parts: one concerned with the execution of individuals, the other with establishing systems of punishment that incorporate the death penalty. If, in an effort to resolve these issues, approaches such as those examined in chapters 1, 4, and 5 are appealed to, then—because of defects in those approaches—the issues are unlikely ever to be satisfactorily resolved. Moreover, they will remain unresolved in the case of capital punishment for reasons just like those that apply to punishment in general. On the other hand, if the societal-defense account of punishment developed here offers genuine hope for solving the justification problem for punishment in general, then it also indicates how to approach the problem of justifying capital punishment.

Although the justification of capital punishment is but one component of a larger issue, it has traditionally received special attention from philosophers. Perhaps for this reason there is the danger that important lessons learned from investigating the justifiability of punishment in general will be forgotten in discussions of capital punishment. In particular, discussions of capital punishment might fail to pay sufficiently close attention to the distinction between justifying individual punishment and justifying systems of punishment. While reasonable people might disagree about how to approach these two components of the

131

justification problem, there can be no doubt that the components are importantly different and that the difference between them must be attended to in discussions of capital punishment.

A second distinction that might receive less attention than it deserves in discussions of capital punishment is that between principled (or theoretical) and practical questions regarding the establishment of systems of punishment that incorporate the death penalty. Principled justifications are concerned with whether capital punishment is necessarily wrong—wrong by its very nature. Practical justifications, on the other hand, deal with questions about whether the death penalty is morally objectionable in particular circumstances by virtue of the contingent features of those circumstances and about whether incorporating the death penalty in some existing system of punishment is justified. If, for example, "life is sacred" in the sense that everyone has an absolute right to life—and if this is necessarily true—then capital punishment is unjustified in principle. Suppose, however, that capital punishment is justified in principle. Suppose further that considerations of deterrence are relevant to whether punishment in general is justified. Then whether capital punishment is justified in particular circumstances depends on whether it is in fact an effective deterrent in those circumstances.

The situation here is, of course, exactly analogous to that which obtains in the area of individual self-defense. That is, one might ask on the one hand whether and, if so, why homicide in self-defense is justified in principle; or one might ask on the other hand whether and, if so, why some particular act of self-defense is justified. Principle J provides an answer to the first of these questions, but applying J to some actual situation in order to determine whether a particular act of homicide in self-defense is justified requires factual information about that situation. The requisite information would pertain to such things as whether the situation in question involves a choice that is forced in the relevant sense, whether a defensive act less severe than homicide would be equally effective in preventing the death of an innocent person, and so on.

How theoretical questions about the morality of capital punishment should be answered will, of course, affect the relevance of proposed answers to practical questions in this area. Thus, if the societal-defense account is correct, then information about the deterrent value of including the death penalty in a system of punishment is relevant to whether that system is morally acceptable. Not all information about deterrent value, however, is given relevance by the societal-defense view. In particular, the number of murderers executed versus the number of potential murderers deterred is irrelevant on the societal-defense account—as is analogous information irrelevant in the case of individual self- and other-defense. Although our initial concern here is with the justifiability of capital punishment in principle, any conclusions we draw will bear importantly on practical matters. Some of these matters will be addressed later in this chapter.

To the extent that questions of principle are given special attention in discussions of capital punishment, they are typically addressed in connection with claims and queries regarding the relevance of considerations of desert or of deterrent value to the morality of capital punishment. The idea that capital punishment might profitably be thought of as somehow analogous to homicide in self- or other-defense is either ignored entirely or briefly mentioned only in passing. Hugo Adam Bedau is something of an exception to this rule, however, and his discussion of what he calls a ''social defense'' account of capital punishment warrants some attention here.[1]

Bedau begins his discussion with these remarks.

> Capital punishment, it is sometimes said, is to the body politic what self-defense is to the individual. If the latter is not morally wrong, how can the former be? To assess the strength of this analogy, we need first to inspect the morality of self-defense.[2]

Bedau then proceeds with this inspection, emphasizing the relevance to the morality of self-defense of considerations much like those embodied in our proportionality and minimization conditions for J.[3] He also invokes a principle that bears a strong—although perhaps only superficial—resemblance to J. The principle is that

> if a life is to be risked, then it is better that it be the life of someone who is guilty (in this context, the initial assailant) rather than the life of someone who is not (the innocent potential victim). It is not fair to expect the innocent prospective victim to run the added risk of severe injury or death in order to avoid using violence in self-defense to the extent of possibly killing his or her assailant. Rather, fairness dictates that the guilty aggressor ought to be the one to run the risk.[4]

So far so good, but Bedau never actually considers the applicability of his principle to punishment, and he does not do what he says he must—namely, ''assess the strength of'' the analogy between self-defense and punishment. As we noted earlier, although J can be used to justify punishment as a general practice, it is inapplicable to cases of individual punishment, and the same might be true of Bedau's principle. Indeed, Bedau does not clearly distinguish the problem of justifying the execution of individuals from questions about including the death penalty in systems of punishment.

Bedau's examination of punishment as social defense also suffers from his evident assumption that applying the social defense approach to the problem of capital punishment requires cost/benefit analyses of capital punishment—analyses that Bedau claims fall far short of establishing that executing criminals is morally justified. If social defense is indeed analogous to individual self-defense, however, then cost/benefit analyses are appropriate in the former area only if they are appropriate in the latter; and we have found very good reasons to doubt that the costs and benefits of defending oneself from wrongful aggression are relevant to the morality of self-defense.[5]

Similar remarks apply to Bedau's treatment of the question, "How many guilty lives is one innocent life worth?"[6] If this question is appropriately asked in the context of examining the morality of capital punishment, then—if social defense and self-defense are analogous—the question is also appropriate in discussions of the morality of individual self-defense, and yet the question is *not* appropriate when asked in connection with self-defense, since numbers of wrongful aggressors versus numbers of innocent potential victims have no bearing on whether self-defense is justified.

These criticisms of Bedau's account are not directed at his conclusion—at his claim that, in circumstances even remotely resembling those obtaining in the actual world, capital punishment is not justifiable on grounds of social defense. The questions raised above concern the reasons Bedau offers for this conclusion—reasons that reflect an incomplete, and perhaps mistaken, view of the moral dimensions of individual self-defense.

Let us now consider how the analogy between social (or societal) defense and self-defense might correctly be used in addressing the question of whether capital punishment is justifiable. Note that our concern here is with the justifiability of capital punishment in principle. To determine whether capital punishment is justified in practice, we would need information of a sort that no theory of punishment is capable of delivering. Given that the societal-defense view applies directly to systems of punishment and only indirectly to individual punishment, the task before us is to explain the relevance of considerations of societal-defense—and hence of the considerations embodied in J—to the justifiability of including the death penalty in systems of punishment.

It is surely possible, and not merely logically or metaphysically possible, that harm is distributed more justly within society S if S establishes a system of punishment P that includes the death penalty than if S establishes a system that does not incorporate capital punishment. Moreover, the harm done to criminals by executing them is certainly proportional to the harm done to innocent members of S by certain criminal acts—by acts of murder, for example, and any punishment short of the death penalty for murder could result in a less just distribution of harm among S's members than that which would result from treating murder as a capital offense. Hence, J's proportionality condition would be satisfied by P if capital punishment were restricted to acts of murder within that system, and J's minimization condition could be satisfied if murders were punishable by death. Finally, since including the death penalty in P need not result in harm to innocent persons—by inciting violence, for example—P's side-effect condition could be satisfied.

Do these results constitute a principled justification for incorporating the death penalty in systems of punishment? The answer to this question depends largely on whether the analogy proposed here between societal-defense and individual self-defense really does obtain, because defending oneself against wrongful aggression is clearly justified in principle under certain conditions. The problem in this area is to produce the principle that explains why and when individual self-defense is justified. If our principle J satisfactorily serves this purpose and if it also applies to situations in which societies are faced with certain forced choices regarding the establishment of systems of punishment, then individual self-defense is indeed appropriately analogous to punishment as societal-defense. If J provides a principled justification for homicide in self-defense under certain conditions, then it also provides a principled justification for systems of punishment that include the death penalty under analogous conditions.

Having argued that punishment as societal-defense provides a principled justification of capital punishment, we can now address the question of whether capital punishment is justified in practice—whether any actual society is justified in including the death penalty on its list of punishments. A practical justification would, of course, require determining how the society's legalizing the death penalty would affect the distribution of harm in that society. Questions about the deterrent value of capital punishment would clearly arise at this point, and they would be no easier to answer in this context than in connection with deterrence theories of punishment, but, as we have noted, these questions about deterrence are not the same in both contexts. In particular, straightforward cost/benefit analyses—while appropriate when applying deterrence theories—have no place in applications of the societal-defense view.

Although we have already emphasized the importance of distinguishing justifications of individual punishment from justifications of systems of punishment, we will do so again here because the distinction is so often ignored when the morality of capital punishment is at issue. For example, people who protest executions of convicted murderers almost invariably ask what good the executions will do, pointing out that they will certainly not bring the murder victims back to life and will therefore result in a net increase in lives lost. Such questions and claims about the consequences of executing individuals are simply inappropriate from the standpoint of punishment as societal-defense, however. The proper practical questions to raise concern the justifiability of establishing particular systems of punishment that incorporate the death penalty. If establishing some such system is indeed justified and if an individual who is guilty of a capital offense is sentenced to death within that system, then executing the individual is, at least presumptively, justified regardless of whether the execution "does anyone any good."

Of course, even if a system of punishment containing the death penalty justly distributes harm by deterring people who would otherwise commit acts such as murder, the justifiability of establishing or retaining the system depends on whether it satisfies J's minimization condition. If, for example, replacing the death penalty with a lesser punishment would result in an equally just distribution of harm, then this counts as a reason for excluding capital punishment from the system. The question of whether a particular system of punishment incorporating the death penalty satisfies the minimization condition is therefore an additional component of the problem of justifying capital punishment in practice.

Although we cannot make much progress here in answering practical questions about the morality of capital punishment, some of these questions are not purely practical in nature. Answering them requires resolving theoretical issues over and above those involved in formulating a theory of punishment. We will now consider two particularly important and related questions that fit into this category. The questions, which, as we shall see, concern matters of justice touched on in chapter 3, are these:

(1) Suppose that some individual guilty of a capital offense in a particular jurisdiction is sentenced to death, while others guilty of the same offense in that jurisdiction are given lesser sentences. Suppose further that this difference in sentencing is due to the influence of racial factors. Does it follow that the individual who is sentenced to death is treated unjustly irrespective of the nature of his offense, the justice of the sentencing laws in the jurisdiction in question, and so on?

(2) Should the death penalty be eliminated from systems of punishment within which sentencing decisions are influenced by racial considerations?

Capital Punishment and Discrimination

In Fulton County, Georgia, in 1978, a man named Warren McCleskey was convicted of murdering a police officer and was sentenced to death for his crime. McCleskey was black and his victim was white, and his conviction was appealed on the ground that imposition of the death penalty in Georgia during that period was influenced by racial considerations and therefore violated Eighth and Fourteenth Amendment Constitutional protections. A key component of the appeal was a report called the Baldus Study, which provided statistical evidence of racial influences on sentencing patterns in Georgia at the time McCleskey was convicted. McCleskey's appeal ultimately reached the United States Supreme Court in 1986 and was denied the following year.

Needless to say, both McCleskey's appeal and the Court's majority opinion are extremely complex, with each citing a multitude of factors in support of its conclusion. Certain components of each are worth mentioning at this time, however. Specifically, the appeal challenged neither the guilty verdict in the McCleskey case nor the legitimacy of the death penalty per se as punishment for crimes like the one of which McCleskey was convicted. The appeal did contend that executing McCleskey would be cruel and unusual, but its emphasis was on the punishment being arbitrary, capricious, and discriminatory—not on its being inhumane or uncivilized. As for the ruling, it did not dispute either the information contained in the Baldus Study or the claim that it provided some evidence of racial influences in sentencing for capital crimes in Georgia. Rather, the Court's majority insisted on the need to demonstrate the presence of certain sorts of racial factors in the sentencing of McCleskey, and it denied that the Baldus Report succeeded in doing so.

Not surprisingly, the McCleskey decision has been the target of vehement criticism from a number of quarters. For example, according to Anthony G. Amsterdam, who joined in the briefs that supported McCleskey's appeal to the Supreme Court,

> Insofar as the basic principles that give value to our lives are in the keeping of the law and can be vindicated or betrayed by the decisions of any court, they have been sold down the river by a decision of the Supreme Court of the United States less than a year old.
>
> I do not choose by accident a metaphor of slavery. For the decision I am referring to is the criminal justice system's *Dred Scott* case. It is the case of Warren McCleskey. . . .[7]

Amsterdam summarizes the Baldus Study's results in support of his denunciation. Additionally, he points out that, of the eleven murderers executed in Georgia between 1973 and 1987, nine were black, and ten of the eleven had white victims; and that, while McCleskey was one of seventeen people found guilty of murdering police officers in Fulton County between 1973 and 1980, only he was sentenced to death for the crime.

Now, if several defendants are all found guilty of the same crime, then it seems clear that—in the absence of relevant differences in the circumstances surrounding those crimes—all the guilty parties should receive the same punishments. This apparently follows from a principle of justice that we encountered in chapter 2, and that is evidently beyond dispute. The principle—referred to earlier as J1, but which we will now call the "comparative principle"—is that justice requires the similar treatment of relevantly similar cases—and the dissimilar treatment of relevantly dissimilar cases). Assuming this principle applies to the McCleskey case, it implies that his being sentenced to death while others convicted of the same crime were not is unjust unless his crime differed in relevant respects from those of the other convicted murderers. If the central claims of McCleskey's appeal are correct, however, then the salient difference between McCleskey's case and the others is most certainly not relevant to whether he should have been sentenced to death, because, according to the appeal, McCleskey was treated differently from other convicted murderers because of his race.

The data cited in support of McCleskey's appeal have also been utilized in arguments aimed at establishing more general conclusions regarding the injustice of capital punishment. These arguments are typically quite straightforward and proceed along these lines: As actually practiced in at least some jurisdictions, capital punishment is unjust because racial considerations influence sentencing decisions in those jurisdictions; unjust practices ought to be abolished; hence, capital punishment ought to be eliminated from the jurisdictions in question. Note that this argument offers a practical, rather than a principled, objection to capital punishment—a reason for excluding the death penalty from systems of punishment in jurisdictions where certain racial influences are in fact present. Note too that this argument attempts to show that systems of punishment like that which existed in Georgia during the 1970s and 1980s should be abolished (or at least modified in certain ways), not that some individual—Warren McCleskey in particular—should not be executed.

So, two different arguments can be seen as arising from the McCleskey case. One is aimed at showing that McCleskey's sentence was unjust, and the other attempts to demonstrate the injustice of the system of punishment within which McCleskey was sentenced, an argument that would of course apply to relevantly similar systems of punishment. It appears, moreover, that both arguments contain the same central premise: that sentencing in capital cases in Georgia during the time McCleskey was tried and convicted was influenced by racial factors. If this premise is indeed central to both arguments, then one can see why some supporters of McCleskey's appeal have claimed that evidence of a pattern of racial discrimination in capital cases in Georgia is evidence of racist influences in particular cases.

We will consider the two arguments separately, beginning with the one concerning McCleskey's case and leaving for later an examination of the argument aimed at showing that certain sorts of systems of punishment are unjustified in practice. We will see then that, although the two arguments might seem to stand or fall together, they are in fact independent of each other in very significant respects.

Let us begin by looking more closely at the idea that McCleskey was treated unjustly because racial influences led to his receiving a sentence more severe than those imposed on others guilty of similar offenses. In doing so we will assume that McCleskey's crime was indeed a capital offense under Georgia law and that the law itself was not unjust—assumptions that, as we have observed, are not challenged in McCleskey's appeal. Under these assumptions, however, McCleskey's sentence was not racially influenced in ways that resulted in an incorrect conclusion regarding how he should be sentenced—a conclusion at odds with the law's dictates. At worst, those involved in sentencing McCleskey arrived at the right decision for the wrong reasons. Granted, if one knew only that the sentencing jurors in McCleskey's case were racially motivated, then one might have reason to suspect that their decision was incorrect, but much more than this is known about the case, and what is known gives no indication that McCleskey's sentence was incorrect—or even a close call, over which reasonable and informed people might disagree.

To be sure, if those involved in the sentencing decision were led to their conclusion by racist attitudes rather than by the evidence presented to them, then they failed in their obligation to base their decision on the factors stipulated as relevant by Georgia's sentencing laws. Moreover, if the individuals in question were indeed motivated by racist attitudes, then they were morally flawed. None of this, however, implies that the *sentence* they imposed was morally flawed by virtue of being an injustice to McCleskey. If race played a relevant role in sentencing in capital cases in Georgia, this was in the cases of any whites who were guilty of capital offenses under Georgia law, but who were given lesser sentences for racial reasons. If there were such cases, then the role of racial factors would be relevant in them because these factors influenced jurors to arrive at incorrect decisions. So there is reason to regard the Court's insistence on showing the presence of racial influences on McCleskey's sentencing as misplaced.

More importantly, if the justice of McCleskey's sentence turns on whether he was treated differently from relevantly similar individuals, then the issue can presumably be resolved without any consideration of whether racial considerations influenced his or anyone else's sentencing. All that would need to be shown is that others whose crimes were punishable by death under Georgia law were given lesser punishments—and this regardless of why relevantly similar cases were treated dissimilarly.

This point can be approached from a slightly different direction. Suppose that only this much were known about McCleskey's and certain other cases: all the cases satisfy conditions that call for the death penalty under Georgia law—a law that is not itself morally objectionable, and McCleskey was sentenced to death while all the others received lesser penalties. This information is sufficient by itself to imply that, although McCleskey's case is relevantly similar to the others, his was treated differently—which, assuming the applicability of the comparative principle, implies that he was treated unjustly. Now, information about racial influences might explain why the cases in question were treated differently. It might also provide reasons for regarding the judges and jurors in all the cases as racists and for concluding that those in the cases other than McCleskey's failed in their obligations to follow Georgia law, but information about racial influences is in itself not needed to conclude that McCleskey was treated unjustly according to the comparative principle.

This issue regarding the relevance of comparative considerations to matters of justice in sentencing is even more complex than the preceding discussion suggests, however, because we have assumed without question that, if two individuals who are guilty of relevantly similar offenses receive different sentences, then—according to the comparative principle—the one receiving the more severe sentence is treated unjustly. Nothing in the comparative principle, however, warrants this conclusion. All the comparative principle implies is that, if the two are indeed relevantly similar and are treated differently, then an injustice is done. To be sure, someone who receives a sentence more severe than she deserves is treated unjustly, but the proposition that this person is treated unjustly in receiving an undeservedly severe sentence is noncomparative in character and is derivable without considering how others are treated. The way some other, relevantly similar defendant is treated might, of course, provide evidence that the first person has indeed received an undeservedly severe sentence, but the fact that comparative considerations can play this sort of evidentiary role implies nothing at all about the relevance of the comparative principle to matters of justice in sentencing.[8]

Notwithstanding the presence of these complexities and irrespective of how they should be dealt with, it does seem clear that, if the comparative principle applies to McCleskey's case, then his sentence was indeed unjust. One might therefore expect that those who regard McCleskey as having been treated justly would deny that comparative considerations are relevant to whether individuals are justly sentenced. In particular, one might expect that, in formulating their arguments, the Court's majority would reject the relevance of comparative considerations to whether McCleskey was justly sentenced. In fact, however, there is no reason to think that they did and some reason to think they did not. The precise nature of their position regarding the relevance of comparative considerations is by no means clear, however.

One source of unclarity are claims contained in the ruling about the legitimate exercise of *discretion* by those responsible for applying sentencing statutes. Here is a sampling of these claims.

Implementation of . . . [criminal laws prohibiting murder] necessarily requires discretionary judgments. Because discretion is essential to the criminal justice process, we would demand exceptionally clear proof before we would infer that the discretion has been abused. The unique nature of the decisions at issue in . . . [the McCleskey case] also counsels against adopting such an inference from the disparities indicated by the Baldus study.[9]

. . . our decisions since *Furman* have identified a constitutionally permissible range of discretion in imposing the death penalty.[10]

. . . [McCleskey] cannot base a constitutional claim on an argument that his case differs from other cases in which defendants *did* receive the death penalty. On automatic appeal, the Georgia Supreme Court found that McCleskey's death sentence was not disproportionate to other death sentences imposed in the state. The Court supported this conclusion with an appendix containing citations to 13 cases involving generally similar murders.[11]

At most, the Baldus study indicates a discrepancy that appears to correlate with race. Apparent disparities in sentencing are an inevitable part of our criminal justice system. . . . Where the discretion that is fundamental to our criminal process is involved, we decline to assume that what is unexplained is invidious.[12]

These remarks appear to presuppose that comparative considerations are indeed relevant to the justice of sentencing decisions, while denying that sufficient grounds exist for concluding that McCleskey was treated differently from relevantly similar defendants. More specifically, the remarks seem to imply that applying sentencing statutes is a very imprecise business unavoidably requiring the exercise of discretion; that, within certain limits on the exercise of this discretion, sentencing decisions are not open to challenge; and that these limits were not exceeded in the McCleskey case.

These questions about discretion and its limits (discretion across similar cases, that is) don't even arise, however, if—as some writers have claimed—comparative considerations are entirely irrelevant to whether particular individuals are justly sentenced. According to Ernest van den Haag, for example,

Regardless of constitutional interpretation, the morality and legitimacy of the . . . argument [against capital punishment] regarding capriciousness, discretion, or discrimination, would be more persuasive if it were alleged that those selectively executed are not guilty. But the argument merely maintains that some guilty, but favored, persons or groups escape the death penalty. This is hardly sufficient for letting others escape it. On the contrary, that some guilty persons or groups elude it argues for *extending* the death penalty to them.

Justice requires punishing the guilty—as many of the guilty as possible—even if only some can be punished, and sparing the innocent—as many of the innocent as possible, even if not all are spared. Morally, justice must always be preferred to equality. It would surely be wrong to treat everybody with equal injustice in preference to meting out justice to some. Justice cannot ever permit sparing some guilty persons, or punishing some innocent ones, for the sake of equality. . . .[13]

The idea that comparative considerations are irrelevant to whether individuals are justly punished is also implicit in our earlier remarks about the justification of individual capital punishment and in our more general discussion of individual punishment in chapter 3, because we implied this: if establishing a system containing the death penalty is justified and if an individual who is guilty of a capital offense is sentenced to death within that system, then the sentence is just. This statement says nothing about the need to compare how such an individual is treated with how others are treated within the given system of punishment.

We can see, then, that the question of how precisely to take comparative considerations into account when considering the justice of sentencing decisions is very complex, and its answer is not at all obvious. We have also distinguished two ways in which the issues here might be approached: one stresses the significance of individual guilt and supports the Court's ruling on the McCleskey case; the other emphasizes the importance of comparing McCleskey's sentence with those imposed on other, similarly situated criminals and opposes the Court's ruling.

Resolving the issue of whether comparative considerations are relevant to matters of justice in sentencing is absolutely essential to determining whether McCleskey was justly sentenced, and resolving this issue will require answering some very general and fundamental questions about the nature of justice.

Comparative and Noncomparative Justice

These fundamental questions about justice reflect a traditional concern about the relevance of two very different sets of considerations to whether individuals are treated justly. On the one hand justice is associated with the concepts of equality, similarity, and proportionality, and in this area justice is essentially comparative: whether an individual has been treated justly depends on how his treatment compares with that received by others. On the other hand we have the idea that justice consists in giving everyone "her due," and here justice is not comparative: whether an individual receives just treatment depends on features of that individual and is independent of how others are treated.

Although most contemporary writers on the subject of justice discuss members of these two sets of considerations, few if any deal adequately with both. Indeed, we observed in chapter 3 that there appear to be distinct preferences among some philosophers for either a comparative or a noncomparative approach to explaining the concept of justice, and these preferences show through in the various accounts of this concept that appear in the literature. We noted, for example, that S. I. Benn and R. S. Peters regard like treatment as the essence of justice, while John Hospers claims that justice consists in treating people according to their deserts. We also observed that some discussions of justice—William Frankena's for one—contain both comparative and noncomparative elements.

As Joel Feinberg has pointed out, the idea that justice is comparative is reflected in the requirement that relevantly similar cases be treated similarly and relevantly dissimilar cases be treated dissimilarly—which is, of course, our comparative principle. In contrast, the idea that justice is noncomparative is embodied in the requirement that individuals be treated in accordance with their rights and deserts (which we will call the "noncomparative principle").[14] As was noted above, the comparative principle appears to provide firm grounds on which to oppose the *McCleskey* decision; while those who regard the decision as correct are likely to base their view on the noncomparative principle. In any case, we will be focusing on the idea that, if McCleskey was unjustly sentenced, then the injustice was comparative in character: the comparative principle was violated—relevantly similar cases were treated dissimilarly—when McCleskey was sentenced to death while others guilty of equivalent offenses were not.

The cases of interest to us here therefore have this feature in common: some individuals escape deserved burdens while others do not. Before examining these cases, which will be called "burden deficit" or BD cases, we will find it useful to consider some cases to which they are similar in regard to the applicability of the comparative principle. In these other cases, individuals are accorded benefits beyond those of which they are deserving.[15]

For example, suppose that on a friend's birthday you give her something you know she wants very much, but that you give nothing to another friend of yours on his birthday. If the comparative principle applies to this case and if your friends are relevantly similar, then your treating them differently is an injustice—and presumably an injustice to the person who receives no gift, but, while there might be something wrong with your treating your friends differently—or something wrong with you for treating them differently—you do nothing that is unjust. By its very nature, gift-giving falls outside the realm of justice—because the practice has absolutely nothing to do with rights or deserts. A corollary of this line of reasoning is that, when gift giving is at issue, there is no plausible way in which to characterize the actual or potential recipients of the gifts as *relevantly* similar. Hence, the comparative principle is inapplicable to the situation in which you selectively bestow gifts on your friends.

Gift-giving cases are not occasions for comparative justice because gift giving has nothing to do with rights and deserts. These cases are not, however, the only ones in which individuals are accorded benefits beyond those that they deserve, and some of these other cases seem to be related to rights and deserts in ways that gift-giving cases are not. Thus, consider the following example.

Owner decides to establish a wordprocessing service, and, in an effort to recruit the very best employees, she offers to pay $25 an hour to those who are hired. Not surprisingly, Owner is deluged with applications for the available positions, because (we will assume) even though employment opportunities for people with wordprocessing skills are plentiful and even though the standard hourly wage for people with such skills is quite high, it is far less than $25. Owner carefully scrutinizes the many applications she receives and hires the most qualified of those who apply. The people she hires work out so well that Owner's business thrives, and her profits soar. Indeed, her income is so high that she decides to share the wealth with her employees—with *some* of her employees, that is. Here is one way in which she might do this.

Scenario One

Owner increases the wages of some—but not all—to $30 an hour. Moreover, she does so not because some of her employees are more diligent or productive than others; indeed, those in her employ are all very similar in these respects. Rather, she selects those who receive raises by drawing names from a hat.

Now, assuming that the conditions of initial employment for all the employees are the same, then this scenario certainly seems to involve a violation of the comparative principle because Owner's employees are relevantly similar and are treated differently. Is it, however, at all reasonable to conclude that Owner has acted unjustly in selectively benefiting her workers, given that the rest are still being paid a much higher wage than is fair for the work they are doing?

An affirmative answer to this question would presumably presuppose that the issue here concerns what people are paid for their work, together with the idea—emphasized above—that when wages are at issue, people who are similarly diligent, similarly productive, and so on are relevantly similar, but there is reason to question the first of these presuppositions, namely, the idea that our example is about *wages*. We will be aided in pursuing this issue by considering some alternatives to scenario one. We will continue to assume, however, that the employees are similarly diligent, similarly productive, and so on, and that those who are selectively benefited are chosen by lot.

Scenario Two

Rather than increasing the wages of some of her employees, Owner presents some—but not all—of them with television sets on their birthdays.

Scenario Three

Owner selects certain employees, multiplies the number of hours each worked during a particular period by $5, and presents the resulting amounts of money to the employees on their birthdays.

Now, Owner's actions in scenario two surely count as gift giving and this notwithstanding her being related to the recipients of the television sets as employer to employee. This result is unchanged by assuming that the benefits selectively bestowed by Owner on her employees are in the form of cash rather than electronic equipment. Hence, the sums of money selectively bestowed on the employees in scenario three are also gifts. Since the comparative principle is inapplicable to gift giving, Owner does not treat any of her employees unjustly by selectively benefiting them in the ways described in scenarios two and three.

If we compare scenario three with scenario one, we will see that in the latter each lump sum selectively bestowed on an employee is divided into some number of equal portions that are distributed over a certain time period. This difference is irrelevant, however, to whether the sums of money distributed in scenario one should be regarded as gifts and as therefore outside the purview of comparative justice. Since

Owner's actions in scenario three count as gift giving, moreover, then so do her actions in scenario one. Hence, contrary to the tentative suggestion offered above, Owner does not treat relevantly similar cases dissimilarly in scenario one, because this scenario involves gift giving, and the notion of relevant similarity has no application in gift-giving contexts.

The preceding remarks suggest that, when someone receives more of a good thing than she deserves, then her situation is outside the realm of comparative justice. The point of discussing these "surplus benefit" cases is to weaken the comparative principle's hold on our thinking about distributive justice, so that our examination of burden deficit (BD) cases—particularly those in which individuals receive less severe sentences than they deserve—will be less likely to be influenced by mistaken preconceptions about justice in the distribution of benefits and burdens.[16]

Although our primary concern is with BD cases having to do with sentencing for capital crimes, we will find it useful to begin by considering a somewhat different sort of BD case.

Sheriff, a law enforcement officer, is faced with many standard other-defense situations, as these are characterized in chapter 2. That is, Sheriff often faces situations in which the only way he can prevent innocent people from being killed at the hands of culpable aggressors is by killing the aggressors. Sheriff does not always try to prevent the deaths of those who are the targets of aggression in these situations, however. Sometimes he chooses, on the basis of tossing coins, to allow aggressors to kill innocent people.

This case involves burden deficits in that all the aggressors encountered by Sheriff deserve to be killed—deserve to be burdened in a certain way—but some escape the burden.[17] Viewed from one perspective, Sheriff's killing one but not another of the aggressors is an occasion for comparative justice, because it seems that the aggressors are relevantly similar in that they are at fault for the creation of certain forced-choice situations, and that they are treated differently when some are killed while others are not. In this way of thinking, Sheriff acts in a comparatively unjust way in selectively killing aggressors; and, presumably, he does comparative injustices to the aggressors whom he does kill.

Let us now focus, however, on the first other-defense situation in which Sheriff finds himself—the first situation in which he faces a choice between killing a culpable aggressor and allowing the latter to kill some innocent person. Suppose that in this situation Sheriff refrains from killing the aggressor, thereby allowing the innocent person to be killed. Given our account of the morality of other-defense, Sheriff's refraining is immoral. Yet, assuming that the comparative principle is applicable to BD cases, it creates a moral presumption—and a presumption arising from considerations of justice—against Sheriff's killing any aggressors he subsequently encounters in similar other-defense situations. In other words, the comparative principle would presumptively require Sheriff to allow culpable aggressors to kill innocent persons, because he failed to do what was required of him on a particular past occasion.

This result is surely unacceptable. The fact that Sheriff refrained from protecting an innocent person on some occasion—and thereby failed in his obligation to do so—creates no presumption at all against his protecting other innocent persons. If comparative considerations create no moral presumption against Sheriff's killing aggressors in other-defense situations, then his doing so is not comparatively unjust. Hence, our earlier tentative suggestion is mistaken: our "Sheriff" example does not constitute an occasion for comparative justice.

We should note too that this result would be unaffected if we were to assume that Sheriff's decisions whether to defend innocent persons are based not on tossing coins, but on other sorts of considerations. Suppose, for example, that Sheriff's decisions are determined by racial considerations. Suppose in particular that he refrains from killing the first culpable aggressor he encounters because the latter is white. His forbearance in that situation still creates no moral presumption against his killing nonwhite aggressors in other-defense situations he encounters subsequently.

We can now argue in a parallel fashion that the comparative principle is also inapplicable to cases in which some but not all convicted murderers escape the death penalty even though all deserve to be executed. The following example will aid us in formulating this argument.

Judge is responsible for sentencing defendants found guilty of murder in a particular jurisdiction. The laws in that jurisdiction prescribe executions for murders of a particularly heinous sort, when these murders lack features that the laws stipulate as mitigating. Although Judge imposes the death penalty on many of those guilty of capital crimes under the laws in question, she sometimes imposes lesser sentences on such individuals.

Let us suppose that the sentencing laws to which this example refers are part of a justified system of punishment. This assumption corresponds to a feature of the *McCleskey* appeal referred to above: namely, that it raises no objections to the death penalty per se, and argues that

McCleskey was treated unjustly because he was sentenced to death while other, relevantly similar defendants were not. Presumably, if this argument succeeds, then an appropriate analogue, applied to our ''Judge'' example, would succeed as well. Of course, for the arguments to be analogous (and to avoid question-begging), our assumption that the system of punishment in our example is justified does not imply that its implementation is always just. Our concern is with the rules of the system, not with their application.

We will assume, moreover, that the system of punishment within which Judge is operating—including its stipulation of the death penalty for certain categories of crimes—is justified on grounds of societal-defense. Now, by virtue of being justified on these grounds, the system of punishment we are imagining satisfies the minimization condition for principle J, and, by virtue of satisfying this condition, the system in question would distribute burdens less justly if it excluded the death penalty than it does with capital punishment included.

Suppose now that Judge is facing her first sentencing decision for a defendant who is guilty of an offense of the sort for which the system in question prescribes execution. Imagine too that no mitigating factors are present in the given situation. Finally, suppose that Judge decides to sentence the defendant to a punishment less severe than execution. Then our example is a BD case, and if the comparative principle applies to such cases, then it prohibits Judge from sentencing any other defendant to death, even if some defendants are guilty of the most heinous and vicious of murders—murders for which capital punishment is justifiably prescribed on grounds of societal-defense.

Surely, however, Judge's having refrained from sentencing one convicted murderer to death—thereby failing to uphold a just law that she is specially obligated to obey—does not prohibit her from imposing the death penalty on others guilty of the same capital offense. Indeed, Judge's forbearance in the first case does not create even a presumption against her obeying the law in subsequent cases. For if such a presumption were created, then a corresponding presumption would be created in our Sheriff example, and there is certainly no such presumption in the latter case. Nor does Judge's failure to do her duty presumptively prohibit anyone in a comparable position from imposing sentences prescribed for crimes of a certain sort on those convicted of those crimes. Moreover, just as Sheriff's reasons—reasons centering on racial factors, for example—for not killing some culpable aggressors are irrelevant to whether he acts unjustly in killing others, so Judge's reasons for imposing punishments less severe than death on some convicted murderers are irrelevant to whether she acts justly in sentencing others to death.

The proper conclusion to draw, then, is that our "Judge" case no more constitutes an occasion for comparative justice than does our "Sheriff" example. That is, in neither case are individuals treated unjustly on comparative grounds: in neither case is the imposition of deserved burdens unjust in virtue of the burdens being imposed selectively. But this result, which concerns the *actions* characteristic of at least some BD cases, should not be interpreted as implying that the comparative principle has no bearing at all on such cases, because as we shall now see, the comparative principle provides a criterion for evaluating the systems of rules within which the refrainings characteristic of BD cases takes place. Whether these refrainings are justified depends on whether the corresponding systems of rules are justified.

Individual Justice and Systemic Justice

The clearest applications of the concept of comparative justice are to what will be referred to here as "desert systems." The nature and significance of these systems is hinted at in the following remarks by Benn and Peters.

"Desert" is a normative word; its use presupposes a rule having two components: (i) a condition to be satisfied; (ii) a mode of treatment consequent upon it. . . . We cannot estimate desert, therefore, in a vacuum; we must be able to refer to some standard or rule from which "X deserves R" follows as a conclusion.[18]

The main thrust of these remarks is surely correct—at least if the "modes of treatment" referred to are rather specific in nature. Thus, for example, a judgement to the effect that some individual deserves to be fired from his job must be made in the light of rules that apply to the individual in question and that relate a set of activities that count as punishable to another set of activities that count as punishments. The set of punishable activities, the set of punishments, and the relation between members of these sets comprise a "system of punishment." A system of punishment is one kind of desert system; other such systems are systems of reward, systems of compensation, and systems of grading. All these systems are composed of three elements: a set of desert bases (for example, a set of types of actions classified as offenses); a set of treatments (a set of punishments, for example); and a relation "X calls for Y," where X ranges over the desert bases, and Y ranges over the treatments.

Although the statement of Benn and Peters quoted above is basically correct, one of its components is mistaken. For the claim is made that judgements about individual desert (X deserves R) follow as "conclusions" from the rules of desert systems; but this is not so—at least not without the aid of additional premises. One might engage in an activity that belongs among the desert bases of some desert system and might as a result receive the treatment called for by that activity in the given desert system, but one will not *deserve* this treatment unless the system itself is just. While the conditions that determine the justice or injustice of desert systems vary with the nature of these systems, certain conditions apply to a number of common and important kinds of systems.

Consider, for example, systems of punishment, reward, grading, and compensation for work done. In all these systems it is common for the activities in the desert basis and treatment sets to be ordered relative to appropriate properties. For example, the desert bases of systems of punishment will commonly be ordered relative to their gravity, and the treatments of those systems will be ordered according to their severity; the desert bases of systems of compensation for work done will often be ordered according to the skill or responsibility involved, and the treatments, which will usually involve monetary payments, will be ordered according to the amounts of those payments.

At this point we can see the proper place to raise questions of comparative justice and the proper role of the comparative principle, because one mark of a just desert system of the sort being discussed here is that the orderings of the desert basis and treatment sets are preserved by the "calls for" relation: the similarities and dissimilarities that exist among the desert bases of the system are appropriately reflected in the treatments of that system. In other words, just desert systems treat relevantly similar cases similarly and relevantly dissimilar cases dissimilarly. If relevant similarities are treated similarly and relevant dissimilarities are treated dissimilarly in a desert system, there is no further application of this requirement in determining the justice or injustice of individual actions that are the treatments of that system.

As it applies to systems of punishment, for example, the idea that relevantly similar cases should be treated similarly and relevantly dissimilar cases should be treated dissimilarly was equated in chapter 2 with the idea that punishments should fit crimes in the sense of being relatively proportional to crimes. We are now saying this: if relative proportionality obtains in a system of punishment and if the system is otherwise just, then whether an act of punishing that belongs to the system is just will depend on whether the punishment is deserved by the individual on whom it is imposed, without any reference to how others are treated.

Thus, suppose that you are convicted of a crime in some jurisdiction, and that you are sentenced to five years in prison. We will assume that you are guilty as charged, and that the criminal justice system within which you were arrested, tried, and sentenced is a just system (that, in particular, it satisfies the comparative principle in the manner described above). Then, in the absence of mitigating factors, your being imprisoned for five years is just—irrespective of whether other, similarly situated criminals receive lesser sentences. In other words, whether you are treated justly in being sentenced to five years in prison is a noncomparative matter, following from the fact that you deserve that punishment. To be sure, your deserving that punishment depends on your having been tried and sentenced within a just system; and whether the system is just depends partly on comparative considerations. The fact remains, however, that comparisons with the sentences imposed on others have no bearing whatever on the justice of your sentence.

Hence, as was suggested earlier, we must distinguish between the conditions under which acts of punishing, compensating, and so on, are just or unjust, and conditions under which systems of punishment, compensation, and so on, are just or unjust. What is being claimed here is that the comparative principle expresses a requirement that belongs among the latter and not the former set of conditions. The justice of particular actions—at least insofar as it involves matters of desert of the kind we have discussed here—is entirely independent of the comparative principle and is determined noncomparatively in the light of features of the individuals whose treatment is in question. Therefore, at the level of particular actions that involve specific deserved treatments, there is no such thing as a comparative injustice.

Although the point will not be argued here, it is reasonable to extend these conclusions to other desert contexts. If such extensions are indeed legitimate, then questions concerning the justice of individual actions are noncomparative and are arrived at by appealing ultimately to the noncomparative principle and never to the comparative principle, while questions concerning the justice of systems of rules of various sorts are, at least in part, comparative and are answered by appealing to the comparative principle.

We now have a theoretical basis on which to explain why the comparative principle is inapplicable to our "Judge" example. More importantly, we have a theoretical framework within which to address our earlier questions about capital punishment and discrimination. Recall that there were two such questions. One concerned whether Warren McCleskey was treated unjustly in being sentenced to die for his crimes when others guilty of relevantly similar offenses received lesser sentences. The other question we raised is whether the existence of racial influences in sentencing for capital offenses in a particular jurisdiction provides grounds for abolishing capital punishment within that jurisdiction.

Given what has been concluded here about the nature and scope of comparative justice, the first question can be answered rather easily. If, as we have claimed, the comparative principle is inapplicable to particular actions, then comparing McCleskey's sentence with that imposed on others cannot be used as a basis for concluding that McCleskey was treated unjustly, regardless of whether any of the sentencing decisions were racially motivated. Indeed, if the system of punishment within which McCleskey was punished satisfied the requirements of the comparative principle and was otherwise just, then (other things being equal—which things do not include comparative considerations) his being sentenced to death was justified.

To be sure, one might well deny that the antecedent of this conditional is true on the grounds that McCleskey was punished within a criminal justice system that—de facto, at least—classified offenses as more or less serious partly on the basis of racial factors. The idea here is that, in the system in question, murders by black people were treated as if they were more serious than murders by white people, and the former were therefore correlated with a more severe punishment than the latter. Since racial considerations are clearly irrelevant to how people should be punished, the system we are discussing treated relevantly similar offenses (murders of a certain type committed under certain conditions) dissimilarly by correlating some with capital punishment and other with lesser penalties, and therefore violated the comparative principle.

Even if this line of reasoning were sound, however, it would not establish that McCleskey was treated *unjustly* in receiving the death penalty. It would only indicate how people who are punished within unjust systems of punishment might themselves be treated justly. Systems of punishment and the criminal justice systems in which they are embedded are very complex entities, and they can be seriously flawed in ways that do not affect the justice of all of their outcomes. This is not, however, to downplay the importance of eliminating injustices—whether de facto or de jure—from systems of punishment, because—McCleskey's case notwithstanding—systemic injustices typically do lead to injustices in the treatment of individuals. Nor are we forgetting that racist attitudes on the part of those who make sentencing decisions are moral defects regardless of whether those attitudes lead to injustices in particular cases. Of course, we should also neither ignore nor underestimate the seriously immoral acts performed by those who allow racial factors to influence their decisions in the sentencing of *whites* who are guilty of capital offenses, and who thereby fail to fulfill their obligations to base their decisions on legally relevant considerations.

The second of our two questions is whether capital punishment should be eliminated from systems whose sentencing decisions are influenced by racial factors. Because this question concerns the justification of a system of punishment in practice, it raises issues of an empirical nature—issues that clearly cannot be resolved here. We can, however, emphasize some points that need to be borne in mind when attempting not only to resolve these empirical issues, but even to identify them.

We noted earlier that—given certain assumptions regarding the legal system within which McCleskey was sentenced—racial factors did not yield an incorrect decision in his case but did do so in cases where others guilty of the same type of offense were given lighter sentences. If this latter sort of role were the only one played by racial factors in a criminal justice system containing the death penalty, then there would appear to be grounds not for eliminating the death penalty from that system, but rather for working toward the elimination of improperly lenient sentences.

The likelihood is vanishingly small, however, that racial influences will take so limited a form in the real world. If in some jurisdiction sentencing decisions in capital cases proceeded systematically along racial lines, then racial factors are bound to influence other aspects of that jurisdiction, and even if Warren McCleskey was not treated unjustly in being sentenced to death while white murderers received lesser sentences, any criminal justice system in which racial considerations played so significant a role is a system in which such considerations would almost certainly play other significant roles as well. They would, for example, influence decisions regarding arrests, arraignments, verdicts, and sentences of non whites in other cases. One could reasonably wonder, then, whether non whites sentenced to death in jurisdictions like the one in question are correctly sentenced—whether, in other words, there is a good chance that people are mistakenly being sentenced to death.

We have in these considerations at least the beginnings of a practical argument for eliminating the death penalty from systems of punishment in which racial factors exert significant influences. Developing the argument further would, of course, require the acquisition of additional information of various sorts and, in light of that information, identifying options, determining the likely outcomes of those options, and so on. The difficulties associated with accomplishing these tasks are clearly enormous, but—fortunately—we need not deal with them here. The point of this discussion has been to explain the relevance of claims about discrimination to questions about the justifiability of capital punishment. As we have seen, such claims are relevant to justice in the punishment of individuals not by virtue of comparisons to punishments imposed on others, but only insofar as they indicate that those individuals have been treated contrary to morally acceptable laws or in accordance with immoral laws. Claims about discrimination are relevant to practical justifications of systems of punishment that include the death penalty insofar as they raise questions about the correctness of imposing death sentences on individuals found guilty of certain sorts of offenses.

Summary

When applied to the problem of capital punishment, punishment as societal-defense indicates sorts of considerations that justice requires be taken into account in determining whether a system of punishment should incorporate the death penalty. The issue here turns on whether systems that contain the death penalty on their lists of punishments will distribute burdens more justly than will similar systems that do not include the death penalty; and on whether the former systems satisfy J's minimization, proportionality and side-effect conditions. Punishment as societal-defense therefore suggests a certain approach to the problem of capital punishment, and it provides a justification in principle. Determining, however, how the problem should be solved in particular societies—determining whether capital punishment is justified in practice—requires answering certain questions about the conditions actually obtaining in those societies.

By and large, answering such questions is beyond the scope of any strictly philosophical inquiry. For example, philosophical investigation alone cannot determine whether an actual system of punishment distributes harm more justly with the death penalty included on its list of punishments or without the death penalty's being included. Even though determining whether capital punishment is justified in practice requires empirical investigation, however, the matter is not entirely empirical in character. For example, in order to answer questions about the moral significance of discriminatory influences on sentencing, certain conceptual issues must be resolved.

These latter issues concern the relevance of comparative considerations to whether wrongdoers are justly sentenced to death. An examination of the nature of justice reveals that comparative considerations have no direct bearing on the justice of capitally punishing individuals but are relevant to the justice of systems of punishment. This relevance obtains by way of the idea that, in just systems, punishments are relatively proportional to crimes. In this latter capacity, comparative considerations are indirectly relevant to the justice of capitally punishing individuals, because the justice of individual punishment depends in part on whether it occurs within just systems.

Despite this connection between the justice of individual punishment and the justice of systems of punishment, individuals who are punished—even capitally punished—within discriminatory systems are not necessarily treated unjustly, but discriminatory systems of punishment are likely to be embedded in legal frameworks so pervaded by discriminatory influences that individual injustices are almost certain to occur.

In conclusion, we should note that remarks made earlier about justifying capital punishment in theory and in practice apply as well to punishment in general. By itself, the theory of punishment as societal-defense cannot determine whether establishing a particular system of punishment—or whether engaging in punishment at all—is in fact justified, but the theory does indicate the sorts of considerations to be taken into account when attempting to make such determinations. These considerations are embodied in principle J, which provides a basis for justly distributing burdens under certain conditions. The relevant conditions obtain in a variety of situations in which individuals are at fault for the creation of risks of harm for themselves or others.

Principle J generates a solution to the justification problem for punishment by providing a framework within which to explain deep-seated and enormously plausible intuitions that almost everyone has regarding the morality of individual self-defense and within which to construct an appropriate analogy between self-defense and societal-defense. Because J incorporates and interrelates forward- and backward-looking considerations, punishment as societal-defense avoids the serious difficulties that plague retributivist and deterrence theories, and by virtue of the analogy between individual and societal-defense, the considerations that justify harming others in self-defense also justify harming people through punishment.

Notes

Introduction

1. See, for example, Hugo Adam Bedau, "Capital Punishment," in Tom Regan, ed., *Matters of Life and Death* (New York: Random House, 1980): 194f; George P. Fletcher, "Punishment and Self-defense," in R. G. Frey and Christopher W. Morris, ed., *Liability and Responsibility* (Cambridge: Cambridge University Press, 1991): 415–30; Stephen Nathanson, *An Eye for an Eye* (Totowa, N. J.: Rowman and Littlefield, 1987): 15–16; and Robert Nozick, *Anarchy, State, and Utopia* (New York: Basic Books, Inc., 1974): 62f, and *Philosophical Explanations* (Cambridge, Mass.: Harvard University Press, 1981): 364.

Chapter 1: Background

1. For criticisms of versions of the no-infringement view, see Warren Quinn, "The Right to Threaten and the Right to Punish," *Philosophy and Public Affairs* 14 (1985): 327–73; and Judith Jarvis Thomson, "Self-defense and Rights," *Findley Lecture* 1976 (Lawrence, Kans.: University of Kansas Press, 1977).

2. The right here is being interpreted as a "claim right." The nature of claim rights and how they differ from other kinds of rights will be explained below.

3. Referring to propositions (1) and (2) in the text, the suggested solution to the problem of contradictions can be briefly explained as follows.

"Obligated" is ambiguous, and the sense it has in (1) differs from its sense in (2). In particular, one of the propositions can refer to a presumptive (prima facie, defeasible) obligation, the other to a strict (actual, indefeasible) obligation. Indeed, a distinction can be drawn not only between strict and presumptive obligations, but also between strict and presumptive permissions and strict and presumptive rights; and the right referred to in (1) as well as the permission to which (2) refers, can be either presumptive or strict.

Suppose now that the right not to be forcibly confined—as well as its implied obligation—are only presumptive. Then affirming the existence of this right is consistent with the proposition that imprisoning particular wrongdoers is permissible—presumptively or strictly.

For a more detailed discussion of the points as issue here, see Phillip Montague, "When Rights Are Permissibly Infringed," *Philosophical Studies* 53, (1988): 347–66.

4. Although the right-to-punish view can be interpreted as a version of the permissible-infringement view, we will see later that it need not be.

For appeals to the idea of a societal right to punish, see, for example, Quinn: 328–34; A. John Simmons, "Locke and the Right to Punish," *Philosophy and Public Affairs* 20 (1991): 311–49; and R. A. Duff, *Trials and Punishments* (Cambridge: Cambridge University Press, 1986): 207f.

5. Deterrence theories might also be interpreted as concerned with punishment's *probable* effectiveness as a deterrent, but we will not consider such alternative formulations here.

6. Discussions of deterrence theories commonly emphasize the differences between preventing people from engaging in wrongdoing and deterring them from doing so. Thus, people who are imprisoned are thereby prevented from engaging in certain sorts of wrongdoing—embezzlement, child molestation, and car theft, for example—by being incapacitated relative to those sorts of wrongdoings. Whether imprisoning people deters them from future wrongdoing—whether imprisoning them appropriately modifies their beliefs and desires—is a different matter, however. While these differences are important for some purposes, they can be ignored here. Indeed, in the discussion that follows, deterrence is interpreted broadly so that it includes prevention.

It is worth mentioning too that, while deterrence theories can include proposals for justifying threats of punishment, theories of justification for threats of punishment are of no interest to us here unless they are related to claims about the justifiability of actual punishments.

7. Act utilitarianism can be characterized in various ways, and it can be conjoined with various theories of value. The central points being made here regarding act utilitarianism (or, rather, the theories of punishment derivable from it), however, are independent of the particular way in which the position is stated. What matters is the forward-looking or consequentialist character of act utilitarianism. Parallel remarks apply to the discussion of rule utilitarianism that follows.

8. Another possible reply to this argument is offered by S. I. Benn in "An Approach to the Problem of Punishment," *Philosophy* 33 (1958): 331. Benn's reply is convincingly criticized by H. L. A. Hart in *Punishment and Responsibility* (Oxford: Oxford University Press, 1968): chapter 6.

9. See, for example, Hart: 9.

10. Jeffrie G. Murphy, *Retribution, Justice, and Therapy* (Dordrecht: D. Reidel Publishing Co., 1979): 229.

11. Murphy, "Retributivism, Moral Education, and the Liberal State," *Criminal Justice Ethics* 4 (1985): 5.

12. Martin P. Golding, *Philosophy of Law* (Englewood Cliffs, N. J.: Prentice-Hall, 1975): 85.

13. Golding: 85.

14. J. L. Mackie, "Morality and the Retributive Emotions," *Criminal Justice Ethics* 1 (1982): 4.

15. Hart: 231.

16. Bedau, "Concessions to Retribution in Punishment," in J. B. Cederblom and William L. Blizek, ed., *Justice and Punishment* (Cambridge, Mass.: Ballinger Publishing Co., 1977): 53.

17. Bedau, "Concessions": 52. Bedau seems simply to be mistaken in maintaining that claims that link punishment's being justified to its being deserved are trivial and can be accommodated by all theories of distributive justice. If such claims imply a necessary connection between justified punishments and deserved punishments, then act utilitarian theories certainly have no room for them. The fact is that references to desert in a theory of punishment significantly affect the nature of the theory. While this might imply that retributivism as we understand it differs importantly from accounts that some writers refer to as retributivism, this is an implication we could live with—particularly given the high profile desert has in the specific retributivist views with which we will primarily be concerned.

18. Murphy, *Retribution*: 229.

19. Murphy, *Retribution*: 229.

20. Murphy, *Retribution*: 229.

21. George Sher, *Desert* (Princeton: Princeton University Press, 1987).

22. Sher: xi.

23. Sher: 7.

24. Sher: 7.

25. In contrast to special obligations, people can have general obligations without having performed any self-obligating acts. Obligations not to harm others are general in this sense. In contrast to special rights, which imply special obligations, general rights imply general obligations. We will have more to say about these distinctions in chapter 5.

26. Like Sher, both Joel Feinberg and John Kleinig regard compensation as routinely deserved when it is owed. Yet, again like Sher, both Feinberg and Kleinig emphasize that people who deserve treatments deserve them by virtue of their character traits or their past acts—neither of which is routinely relevant to the morality of compensation. (See Joel Feinberg, *Doing and Deserving* (Princeton: Princeton University Press, 1970): 58–61, 74–76; and John Kleinig, "The Concept of Desert," *American Philosophical Quarterly* 8 (1971): 71, 73.)

27. But doesn't the person deserve thanks from you; and are you not—in virtue of his deserts—obligated to thank him?

The latter question can best be approached by asking another question: What would your being obligated to thank the person amount to? One possibility is that you are obligated simply to utter certain words; but then the person would deserve simply to have certain things said to him—which clearly seems not to be true. On the other hand, your obligation might be regarded as including your having certain feelings or attitudes, but there are very good reasons to doubt that one can possibly be obligated to have feelings or attitudes on particular occasions. Of course, if you do not feel grateful and express your gratitude to the person, then this reflects badly on you as a person. But this person appraisal is unrelated to any specific obligations that you might have.

So the answer to the compound question initially posed is this: Yes, the person does deserve thanks from you in the sense of a sincere expression of gratitude on your part, but you are not obligated to thank the person in this sense, although if you do not, then you are morally defective in a certain respect.

28. Sher's discussion of how deserts differ from rights (Sher: 199–201) makes a similar point, even though it fails to square well with his claims about deserved compensation.

29. Feinberg: 62.

30. Feinberg: 72.

31. Feinberg: 72.

32. In *Not Just Deserts* (Oxford: The Clarendon Press, 1990), John Braithwaite and Philip Pettit characterize retributivism in terms of deserts that are very close to those we are interpreting as strictly normative. They introduce a kind of requirement called "constraints" and maintain that if X is constrained to accord Y treatment T, then Y has a "warrant" to treatment T; and they imply that the converse is also true ("The warrant is simply the other side of the constraint" (29). They then distinguish those warrants that serve to protect interests from other warrants and they label the former rights and the latter deserts. In their view, then, one's deserts necessarily imply requirements in others.

The Braithwaite-Pettit position, however, is open to the main criticisms that have been directed here against Sher's view. In addition, the idea that deserts and constraints (of a type) are but two sides of a single coin seems vulnerable to clear counterexamples. The fact, say, that someone in a position of authority is duty bound to enforce rules that result in someone else's being punished most certainly does not imply that the person deserves punishment. A more fundamental difficulty with the Braithwaite-Pettit view of desert is discussed in chapter 4, where the idea that judgments of desert are person appraisals rather than act appraisals is developed.

Chapter 2: Defending and Preserving Individuals

1. Nathanson: 15.

2. Nathanson: 16.

3. Thomson: 3.

4. Thomson: 18.

5. Thomson, "Self-Defense," *Philosophy and Public Affairs* 20 (1991): 299.

6. Thomson, "Self-Defense and Rights": 7.

7. Thomson, "Self-Defense and Rights": 9–10.

8. Suzanne Uniacke has also examined the morality of self-defense at some length in *Permissible Killing* (Cambridge: Cambridge University Press, 1994). However, her view is similar to Thomson's in all respects relevant to this discussion. In particular, it is vulnerable to most of the objections that have been raised here against Thomson's account.

9. For a very different interpretation of what forced choices are, see Cheyney Ryan, "Self-defense, Pacifism, and the Possibility of Killing," *Ethics* 93 (1983): 508–24; and Seumas Miller, "Self-defense and Forcing the Choice between Lives," *Journal of Applied Philosophy* 9 (1992): 239–43.

10. It is rejected, for example, by Michael Otsuka in "Killing the Innocent in Self-defense," *Philosophy and Public Affairs* 23 (1994): 74–94.

It is worth noting that self- and other-defense cases with innocent bystanders present special difficulties when they involve culpable aggressors as well. In such cases one's presumptive right to kill a culpable aggressor might not be a right, all things considered, if killing the aggressor will also cause the deaths of innocent bystanders.

11. It is important when considering any of the defense or preservation cases discussed here to distinguish questions regarding whether the conditions described in the cases are satisfied from questions about whether anyone *knows* that they are satisfied. These latter questions are being ignored throughout this discussion—a point that we will have occasion to repeat later in the text.

12. See Nozick, *Anarchy*: 34.

13. Note that the lives of aggressors in P3 cases are not at stake, so they are not in the fields of the choices in those cases.

14. John Locke, "Of Civil Government," (*Second Treatise*), ch. 3.

15. For illuminating discussions of the law of self-defense, see George P. Fletcher, "Proportionality and the Psychotic Aggressor: A Vignette in Comparative Criminal Theory," *Israeli Law Review* 6 (1973); and Sanford H. Kadish, "Respect for Life and Regard for Rights in the Criminal Law," *California Law Review* 64 (1976).

16. As used in principle J, "harm" is being interpreted narrowly, as roughly equivalent to "injury or death." "Harm" can also be construed broadly, however. Under this broad interpretation, harms are invasions of interests and include being at risk of injury or death. (For an explanation of this latter sense of harm, see Feinberg, *Harm to Others* (New York: Oxford University Press, 1984), ch. 1.) Later, the applicability of J will be extended to cases involving forced choices in the distribution of harm where "harm" is broadly construed. This extension seems entirely appropriate: someone forced to choose between placing either of two parties at risk of injury or death is certainly justified in

directing the risk toward the party whose fault it is that she and the other party are at risk, if there is such a party. I should add that throughout the discussion "harm" and "burden" will be used interchangeably.

17. That J applies to this case helps explain how obligations of compensation differ from other obligations that people incur as a result of their own voluntary acts—obligations to keep promises, for example. The applicability of J to compensation cases might provide a basis for claiming that obligations to compensate people for having caused them to suffer losses—as obligations of justice—are properly enforceable by the criminal law, whereas obligations to keep promises, to pay debts, and so on, are not. (In this connection it is important to distinguish between, on the one hand, the reparative obligations people incur when they wrongfully cause others to suffer losses and, on the other hand, obligations of justice—arising from J—that societies might have to establish and enforce legal requirements that such reparative obligations be fulfilled.)

18. Again, see Cheyney Ryan's and Seumas Miller's discussions of forced choices in the articles referred to above.

Chapter 3: Societal-Defense

1. John Rawls, *A Theory of Justice* (Cambridge: Harvard University Press, 1973). Subsequent page references to this work are contained in the text.

2. Rawls's two principles of justice, together with their "Priority Rules," are stated on 302–303. He points out certain problems to which relying on the general conception gives rise, but these problems are not relevant to our discussion of Rawls's account of justice.

3. John Hospers, "Free Enterprise as the Embodiment of Justice," in Richard T. De George and Joseph A. Picher, ed., *Ethics, Free Enterprise, and Public Policy* (New York: Oxford University Press, 1978): 73.

4. S. I. Benn and R. S. Peters, *Social Principles and the Democratic State* (London: George Allen and Unwin, Ltd., 1959): 111.

The Benn and Peters principle resembles J1 in certain respects, but—arguably, at least—the principles are not equivalent to each other, because the former evidently embodies a presumption in favor of equal treatment that is not present in J1. This difference is revealed in part by the fact that—unlike J1—the Benn and Peters principle says nothing about what to do in situations in which individuals are relevantly dissimilar. That is, Benn and Peters do not maintain, for example, that individuals should be treated unequally unless they are similar in relevant respects—a principle that seems to contain a presumption in favor of unequal treatment.

5. William Frankena, "The Concept of Social Justice," in Richard B. Brandt, ed., *Social Justice* (Englewood Cliffs, N.J.: Prentice-Hall, 1962): 9.

6. Frankena: 9.

7. Frankena: 10–11. Frankena's characterizing justice sometimes as com-

parative, at other times as noncomparative, echoes what appears to be a similar ambivalence on the part of Aristotle, who claims that "We have shown that both the unjust man and the unjust act are unfair and unequal. . . . the unjust is unequal, the just is equal, as all men suppose it to be, even apart from argument." (*Nicomachean Ethics*: 1131a.) But Aristotle goes on to say that ". . . all men agree that what is just in distribution must be according to merit in some sense." (1131a)

8. See, for example, James Sterba's discussion of interpretations of justice in *How to Make People Just* (Totowa, N.J.: Rowman and Littlefield, 1988).

9. According to Jenny Teichman, "in the traditional theory [of the just war], self-defense . . . is more or less taken for granted." (*Pacifism and the Just War* (Oxford: Blackwell, 1986): 47). Teichman goes on to claim, "If there is no right of self-defence, there can be no theory of justice in war" (69). In a similar vein Michael Walzer states that "self-defense seems the primary and indisputable right of any political community." (*Just and Unjust Wars* (New York: Basic Books, 1977): 82.)

10. Teichman: 46.

11. See chapter 2, note 16.

12. On this point, see Fletcher, "Proportionality."

13. Quinn, "The Right to Threaten": 337.

14. Quinn: 359.

15. Quinn: 361.

16. See chapter 1, note 4. Subsequent references in this chapter to Duff's book will be contained in the text.

Chapter 4: Rethinking Retributivist and Deterrence Theories

1. Sher: 20.

2. Herbert Morris, "Persons and Punishment," *The Monist* 52 (1968): 477–78.

3. Sher does not accept Morris's evident egalitarianism, and, whereas Sher claims that wrongdoers gain an unfair advantage, Morris depicts them as unfairly avoiding a burden.

4. Sher: 82.

5. Morris: 478.

6. Sher argues, with dubious success, that wrongdoers need not be burdened by those whom they wrong. (On this point see C. L. Ten, "Positive Retributivism," *Social Philosophy and Policy* 7 (1990): 196–200.) In any case, the fact would remain that *legal* punishment is not required by his account.

7. Murphy, *Retribution*: 77.

8. Murphy, *Retribution*: 77.

9. For example, see Murphy's "Retributive Hatred," in R. G. Frey and

Christopher W. Morris, ed., *Liability and Responsibility* (Cambridge: Cambridge University Press, 1991): 351–76.

10. In a more recent discussion Murphy indicates that arguments advanced by Robert Nozick have convinced him that fairness accounts of retributivism are seriously defective. He also suggests that a form of Mackie's negative retributivism is capable of avoiding the problems that afflict deterrence theories. Murphy appears therefore to have espoused a kind of "pluralistic" deterrence theory, a type of account to be discussed later in this chapter. (See Murphy, "Retributivism": 7. Nozick's arguments are presented in *Anarchy*.)

Partly because pluralistic deterrence theories and negative retributivism are themselves objectionable in several important respects, and partly because some might find Nozick's arguments less convincing than Murphy does, we will treat Murphy's fairness account as worthy of consideration despite the doubts he has expressed regarding its viability.

11. Rawls, "Legal Obligation and the Duty of Fair Play," in Sidney Hook, ed., *Law and Philosophy* (New York: New York University Press, 1964): 9–10.

12. Rawls, "Legal Obligation": 17.

13. Rawls, "Legal Obligation": 17.

14. Richard Dagger attempts to rebut the objection to fairness accounts that we are presently discussing, but he fails to consider any of the points just raised. (Richard Dagger, "Playing Fair With Punishment," *Ethics* 103 (1993): 473–88.) Dagger provides no reason at all to believe that many (or any) murderers, rapists, and so on, act contrary to agreements when they commit their crimes. Nor does he argue that, even if some seriously harmful acts are also unfair to those who are harmed, such acts should be punished because they are unfair rather than because they are harmful.

15. Sher: 94.

16. Sher: 94.

17. Sher: 97.

18. The differences between judging persons and judging acts may be blurred if another distinction is not also borne in mind. The latter is between two interpretations of how the moral appraisal of acts should proceed—whether it should be entirely "objective" or should contain at least some "subjective" elements. If the subjectivist view is correct, then the moral status of acts depends on certain facts about their agents' mental lives; and since facts of a similar sort seem relevant to appraising the agents themselves, we might be tempted to infer from the subjectivist account that morally appraising acts somehow involves morally appraising people. This temptation should probably be resisted, however. Even if some version of subjectivism is acceptable, the kinds of mental facts that can plausibly be regarded as relevant to act appraisals might be very different from those relevant to appraising agents. It might be the case, for example, that whether an action with bad consequences is morally wrong depends on whether its agent anticipated those consequences, but that whether the latter is blameworthy for acting depends on whether he acted in

good conscience—on whether he believed he was doing the right thing. The question of whether act appraisals should be understood as partly or entirely subjective will be ignored here. We will simply suppose that whether acts are right, wrong, obligatory, and so on *might* depend upon the beliefs, attitudes, and so forth with which their agents act; although we will also be assuming that, even if the moral status of acts does indeed depend on certain facts about the mental lives of their agents, this does not undermine the distinction between act-appraisal and person-appraisal.

19. Quinn, 328–73. Subsequent references to this article are contained in the text.

20. For a penetrating critique of the second stage of Quinn's justification process (i.e., that concerned with justifying punishments in terms of justified threats of punishment), see Daniel Farrell, "On Threats and Punishments," *Social Theory and Practice* 15 (1989): 125–54.

21. See chapter 1, note 32. Subsequent references to this work are contained in the text.

Chapter 5: Punishment as a Societal Right

1. This sort of view is endorsed in Benn and Peters: 89.

2. Feinberg, "The Nature and Value of Rights," *Journal of Value Inquiry* 4 (1970): 249.

3. For a discussion of this way of thinking about rights, see David Lyons, "Rights, Claimants, and Beneficiaries," in David Lyons, ed., *Rights* (Belmont, Calif.: Wadsworth, 1979): 58–77.

4. Hart, "Are There Any Natural Rights?" *The Philosophical Review* 64 (1955): 188.

5. Some writers would likely attempt to resolve the issues raised by the cases in question by appealing to the idea that your rights are infringed in these cases because your *interests* are adversely affected. This sort of position is unhelpful, however, because there is no end of cases in which interests appear to be adversely affected while no rights are infringed; and the question that remains is why these latter cases do not include examples of the sort we have been discussing.

6. It is worth emphasizing that our sovereignty account of general rights, although centering on the concept of a liberty, nevertheless applies to passive as well as to active rights. Thus, for example, we can make perfectly good sense of the right not to be killed as a component of the right to life, infringements of which occur when individuals contravene obligations of non arrogation by killing others. Indeed, our sovereignty account of rights even accommodates so-called "welfare rights" such as the right to be aided when in distress, although this is not a point that we will pursue here. (For further discussion of this topic,

see Phillip Montague, *In the Interests of Others* (Dordrecht: Kluwer Academic Publishers, 992): ch. 4.)

7. Note that propositions about the morally significant liberties of particular individuals do not in general imply propositions about obligations on the part of others. If, for example, your performing some action would be supererogatory, then you are at liberty in the morally significant sense to perform that action; but others may not be obligated to refrain from interfering with you. Hence, although the morally significant liberties associated with general rights underlie obligations in others, the concept of a morally significant liberty is not *equivalent* to the concept of a general right.

8. For illuminating and interestingly varied discussions of collective responsibility, see Hud Hudson, "Collective Responsibility and Moral Vegetarianism," *Journal of Social Philosophy* 24 (1992): 89–104. Also see the following papers, all of which appear in *Collective Responsibility*, edited by Larry May and Stacey Hoffman (Savage, Md.: Rowman and Littlefield, 1991): "Collective Responsibility" by Joel Feinberg; "Can a Random Collection of Individuals be Morally Responsible?" by Virginia Held; and "Metaphysical Guilt and Moral Taint" by Larry May.

9. Problems surrounding the idea of collective rights are raised by Robert Simon (in "Preferential Hiring: A Reply to Judith Jarvis Thomson," *Philosophy and Public Affairs* 3 (1974): 312–20); and by George Sher (in "Justifying Reverse Discrimination in Employment," *Philosophy and Public Affairs* 4 (1975): 159–170). However, both Simon and Sher focus on problems concerning the relation between the rights of collections on the one hand, and the rights of members of those collections on the other. These problems, while interesting and important, are not the ones we are concerned with here.

10. Some of these difficulties are developed in Simmons's fine treatment of political obligation in *Moral Principles and Political Obligation* (Princeton: Princeton University Press, 1979).

11. Simmons, "Locke": 345. Simmons does not explain what it is for something to be the effective equivalent of a claim right. What he has in mind here is particularly obscure, given how little he says about what claim rights are strictly speaking.

12. Simmons, "Locke": 340.

13. Simmons, "Locke": 338.

14. Simmons, "Locke": 338.

15. Simmons, "Locke": 343.

16. Thus, if there are supererogatory actions, then they are morally good but unrequired; and there might very well be good moral reasons for performing such actions.

17. More generally, arguments are required in support of the idea that claims about a punishments being deserved are relevant to claims about the punishments being justified (for some plausible interpretation of "justified"). Traditional retributivist theories are particularly in need of such arguments, but they

are needed by any account of the justification of punishment that appeals to the notion of desert (as Simmons's account does).

18. The Rossian account of moral presumptions and their defeaters is patterned after a view presented by W. D. Ross in *The Right and the Good* (Oxford: The Clarendon Press, 1930).

19. It is noteworthy that a number of writers who claim to be following Ross in formulating their explanations of the nature and behavior of presumptive moral requirements, and who appear to subscribe to the Rossian view of moral defeaters, seem implicitly to acknowledge the existence of defeaters that are permissive in the sense just described. The views of John Rawls and Robert Nozick are two cases in point.

According to Rawls, supererogatory acts are morally significant and are capable of defeating presumptive requirements to prevent others from being harmed, but he regards these defeaters as functioning very differently from competing presumptive requirements. In particular, they do not by themselves correspond to moral requirements of any kind: they can defeat presumptive requirements without converting to strict requirements. (Rawls, *Justice*: 117, 340f.)

Nozick too seems implicitly to acknowledge the existence of defeaters different from those admitted by the Rossian view. He divides the morally significant features of acts into two sets, those that are "right-making" and those that are "wrong-making." Nozick's right-making features, however, are of two importantly different types: those that correspond to presumptive requirements and carry moral weight by themselves and those whose moral significance consists entirely in their ability to function as moral defeaters. In other words, Nozick's account accommodates two distinct kinds of moral defeaters: the Rossian view's competing presumptive requirements and some that function like those we are calling "permissive." (Nozick, *Explanations*: 479f.)

20. This case might be assimilated to the supererogatory, but whether it should be is unimportant for this discussion.

21. See, for example, John L. Pollock, "A Theory of Moral Reasoning," *Ethics*: 96 (1986): 506–23.

22. Feinberg has posed the question of whether there are "mandatory" rights—rights that their possessors are obligated to exercise. He concludes that such "rights" are

> best understood as ordinary duties with associated half-liberties rather than ordinary claim-rights with associated full liberties, but . . . the performance of the duty is presumed to be so beneficial to the person whose duty it is that he can *claim* the necessary means [to exercise the "right"] from the state and noninterference from others as *his due*. Its character as claim is precisely what his half-liberty shares with the more usual (discretionary) rights and what motivates his use of the word "right" in demanding it. ("Rights": 253)

These remarks are clearly in the same spirit as the position being taken here regarding whether having a right to act is compatible with being required to act.

Note too that this position is derivable from premises having nothing to do with the distinction between presumptive and strict rights, because if the core notion of a claim right is that of a morally significant *liberty*, as the sovereignty account implies, or if claim rights imply liberties (understood as "full permissions"—i.e., as the absence of both obligations to refrain and obligations to act), then a societal right to punish wrongdoers is incompatible with a societal requirement to punish them. Hence, even if the presumptive/strict distinction is unnecessary for the development of a consistent version of the permissible-infringement view (or even if there exists an acceptable version of the no-infringement view), the idea of a societal right to punish might have to be abandoned on the ground that societies are required to punish wrongdoers.

23. Simmons, "Locke": 327, 331; Duff: 200, 207–208.

24. For an excellent discussion of the complexities involved in attempting to develop an acceptable theory of rights, see L. W. Sumner, *The Moral Foundation of Rights* (Oxford: The Clarendon Press, 1987).

Chapter 6: Societal-Defense and Capital Punishment

1. Bedau, "Capital": 160–94.

2. Bedau, "Capital": 177.

3. Bedau also arrives at something like our side-effect condition when he considers the possibility that capital punishment might have an "incitive effect." (Bedau, "Capital": 183.)

4. Bedau, "Capital": 179.

5. The point being made here is similar to one we made in chapter 2, when we noted that Stephen Nathanson regards accounts of punishment that rest on an analogy between self- and societal-defense as deterrence theories. We also noted in chapter 4 that Quinn seems to regard the connection between self-defense and deterrence as much closer than it really is.

6. Bedau, "Capital": 183–85.

7. Anthony G. Amsterdam, "Race and the Death Penalty," *Criminal Justice Ethics* 7 (1988): 2, 84–86.

8. Analogously, determining who wins a race requires comparing the times at which the competitors cross the finish line, but the question of who should receive first prize is determined noncomparatively, and the justice of awarding first prize to one competitor rather than another is independent of how the others are treated.

9. 481 *U.S.* 297 (1986).

10. 481 *U.S.* 305. In its *Furman* decision (408 *U.S.* 238 (1972)), the Supreme Court declared the death penalty unconstitutional when not restricted in certain ways.

11. 481 *U.S.* 278.

12. 481 *U.S.* 313.

13. Ernest van den Haag, "In Defense of the Death Penalty: A Practical and Moral Analysis," in Hugo Adam Bedau, ed., *The Death Penalty in America*, 3rd ed. (New York: Oxford University Press, 1982): 323.

It is noteworthy that, in rejecting (or at least greatly downplaying) the relevance of comparative considerations to the justice of discriminatory influences on capital punishment, van den Haag focuses on matters of *equal* treatment. We, however, have introduced the idea of comparisons by appealing to the comparative principle—to the requirement that relevantly similar cases be treated similarly. These two ways of thinking about comparative considerations are not necessarily equivalent, however—and this not simply by virtue of differences between equality and similarity, because there is no more connection between the comparative principle and a requirement of equal treatment than there is between the comparative principle and a requirement of *un*equal treatment.

14. Feinberg's discussions of these topics are contained in "Noncomparative Justice," *The Philosophical Review* 83 (1974): 297–338; and *Social Philosophy* (Englewood Cliffs, N. J.: Prentice Hall, 1973): 98f.

15. For brevity's sake in the discussion that follows, I will sometimes refer only to deserts when references to rights are also appropriate. Moreover, "desert" will be used very loosely in the present context, so that treatments that are deserved by individuals are simply treatments that are their due or that are otherwise justified. This usage, which ignores distinctions that are important in other contexts (distinctions that were emphasized in previous chapters), will create no problems for the present discussion.

16. For a discussion of other problems associated with applying the comparative principle to particular cases, see Phillip Montague, "Comparative and Noncomparative Justice," *The Philosophical Quarterly* 30 (1980): 131–40.

17. The caveat issued in note 15 is applicable here as well.

18. Benn and Peters: 137.

Index

absolute proportionality thesis, 65–69
accidental threats, 37, 38
act utilitarianism for punishment, 7–9,
    90, 103–104
Amsterdam, Anthony G., 138
Aristotle, 164–65n7
asymmetry problems, 28–31, 34

Bedau, Hugo Adam, 13, 14, 133–34,
    159n1 (Introduction), 161n7,
    170n3
Benn, S. I., 57–58, 144, 150–51,
    160n8, 164n4, 167n1
Braithwaite, John, 101–105, 162n32
burden deficit cases, 144, 147,
    149–50
burdens, distribution of, 43–49, 52,
    55–58, 60; *See also* harm

capital punishment, 2, 25–26,
    131–55; and cost-benefit analyses,
    134; as cruel and unusual, 137; and
    discrimination, 137–43, 153–55;
    practical justification of, 132, 134–
    35, 139, 154–55; principled justi-
    fication of, 132, 135
collective obligations. *See* obligations
collective responsibility, 116
comparative principle, 138, 144–45,
    147–48, 149–50, 151–55, 171n3.
    See also J1, principle
compensation, obligations of. *See* ob-
    ligations

consequentialism, 96–99, 101, 103
correspondence thesis, 65–69

Dagger, Richard, 166n14
defeaters: permissive and prescriptive,
    16, 17, 124–26; rebutting and
    undercutting, 125; Rossian view
    of, 124
desert, 87–90, 126, 150, 168–69n17;
    bases, 19, 150–51, 171n5; loose
    interpretation of, 171n15; systems,
    150–52
deserts, 122–23; strictly normative,
    17–23, 162n32
deterrence theories, 6–11, 26, 90–95;
    distinction between deterrence and
    prevention in, 160n6; pluralistic,
    90–95; utilitarian-based, 6–11,
    74–75, 101
dominion, 101–105
Duff, R. A., 75–76, 128, 160n4

fairness: in John Rawls's theory, 54,
    56, 84–85; in retributivist theories,
    80–90
Farrell, Daniel, 167n20
Feinberg, Joel, 19, 21–22, 111–12,
    144, 161n26, 163n16, 168n8,
    169n22
fighting back, 27–31, 36, 41
Fletcher, George P., 159n1 (Introduc-
    tion), 163n15, 165n12

173

About the Author

Phillip Montague is a Professor of Philosophy at Western Washington University. He has published articles on ethics and social philosophy in a number of journals, including *Philosophy and Public Affairs*, *Philosophical Studies*, and *American Philosophical Quarterly*. He is also the author of *In the Interests of Others: An Essay in Moral Philosophy* (Dordrecht: Kluwer Academic Publishers, 1992).